A Pocket Tour™ of Food & Drink on the Internet

Ellen Gordon and Peter Stokes

San Francisco • Paris • Düsseldorf • Soest

SYBEX

Acquisitions and Development Editor:	Brenda Kienan
Acquisitions Manager:	Kristine Plachy
Editor:	Pat Coleman
Project Editors:	Malcolm Faulds, Laura Arendal
Technical Editor:	Juli Geiser
Book Designer:	Emil Yanos
Desktop Publisher:	Terry Lockman
Production Coordinator:	Nathan Johanson
Indexer:	Ted Laux
Cover Designer:	Joanna Kim Gladden/Design Site
Cover Illustrator:	Mike Miller

Library of Congress Card Number: 95-71029

ISBN: 0-7821-1806-2

Manufactured in the United States of America

10 9 8 7 6 5 4 3 2 1

To Alexandra, who provides food for the soul

Acknowledgments

When we decided to write this book, it seemed like an interesting and exciting project. While it certainly has been that, it has also been a tremendous amount of work—more late nights than we ever could have imagined and a crash course in new and little-known computer error messages.

A number of people deserve our heartfelt thanks; unfortunately, space restrictions allow us to mention only a few.

At Sybex, we owe a debt of gratitude to Brenda Kienan, our developmental editor, for her friendship, patience, and unfailing support whenever we needed it. She remained reassuringly calm and confident at all the right moments. Also thanks to Pat Coleman, our editor, for her enthusiasm, editing skills, and excellent suggestions; to Malcolm Faulds, our long-suffering project editor; and to Juli Geiser, our technical editor. The continuing enthusiasm of all these people, in the face of a demanding project, has been invaluable.

On the homefront, we have to thank our daughter, Alexandra, for her patience and good humor upon hearing for the umpteenth time that we had to work another night or another weekend. Also to unfailing family and friends for their support and patience. To Grandma Esther who offered and delivered on her standing child-care invitation. To Dad and Emilie for their moral support and for providing the hardware to get the job done. To Naomi Yager, Beth Piatnitza, Leah Fortin, Pam Lucker, Kim Walker, Barbara Eddy, and Kathleen Gadway, for their moral support, comic relief, and friendship.

Table of Contents

Appendices

Introduction

The very first time we loaded an Internet Web browser and started it up, we were attracted by the Food and Drink category that was one of the software defaults. After we clicked on Food and Drink, a list of subcategories appeared on the screen, starting with Beer and Brewing and scrolling off the page. Because we really like Mexican food, we immediately moved the cursor to a category called La Comida Mexicana (Mexican food), and there we found a list of recipes, in Spanish, for many of our favorites, organized by category, such as Sopas (soup), Huevos (eggs), Carne (meat), and accompanied by lovely photographs (see Figure I.1).

We were astonished and excited to realize that we had opened up an entire world of culinary possibility that was accessible when we sat down in

Figure I.1:
Mexican food on the Internet

Salsa de chipotle

Ingredientes:

- 1 jitomate grande
- 5 tomates verdes
- - chiles chipotles al gusto
- 1 cebolla picada finamente
- 1 diente de ajo
- 1 cucharada cafetera de vinagre
- - aceite para freír

front of our computer and connected to the Internet. You can even get an English version of this screen by clicking on the phrase _ENGLISH VERSION!_ One of the first things we discovered was not to do this when you're hungry (see Figure I.2).

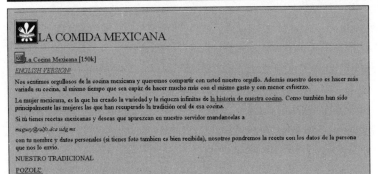

LA COMIDA MEXICANA

La Cocina Mexicana [150k]

ENGLISH VERSION!

Nos sentimos orgullosos de la cocina mexicana y queremos compartir con usted nuestro orgullo. Además nuestro deseo es hacer más variada su cocina, al mismo tiempo que sea capáz de hacer mucho más con el mismo gasto y con menor esfuerzo.

La mujer mexicana, es la que ha creado la variedad y la riqueza infinitas de la historia de nuestra cocina. Como también han sido principalmente las mujeres las que han recuperado la tradición oral de esa cocina.

Si tú tienes recetas mexicanas y deseas que aparezcan en nuestro servidor mandanoslas a

maguey@rulfo.dca.udg.mx

con tu nombre y datos personales (si tienes foto también es bien recibida), nosotros pondremos la receta con los datos de la persona que nos lo envio.

NUESTRO TRADICIONAL

POZOLE

Y

BIRRIA.

* Presiona sobre el platillo deseado.

Figure I.2: Seeing these recipes is enough to make you learn Spanish.

You may not know Spanish or like Mexican food, but if you are interested in getting information and ideas about any kind of food or beverage, in all likelihood it is available somewhere on the Internet, and this book is designed to help you find it. You will find this book useful if you

- like to try recipes and have others try yours.

- want—or need—to get information about a culinary technique or a rare ingredient.

- are interested in exchanging ideas with other folks involved in a similar project or profession.

- like the idea of doing any of the above at your leisure.

WHAT'S IN THIS BOOK

Part One of this book is a general guide to the Internet: an overview, some history about the Internet and its amazing growth, and an examination of the language and terminology you will encounter there. There is also a discussion about what you will need to get started on the Internet: computer equipment (hardware), and computer programs (software), and online services. We provide plenty of hints and tips that will make getting to the fun of being on the Internet as painless as possible.

Part Two is a listing of food and beverage sites on the Internet. It is not complete because our deadline didn't allow time for a 500-page book. Rather, it is a sampling of some of the great sites we found, many of which are themselves guides to other sites. If you are interested in food, as a cook—professional or amateur—or as an eater, once you start to look around at some of the great sources of information out there, you will find it hard to tear yourself away.

HOW TO USE THIS BOOK

To help you understand what sort of site is being discussed, icons appear in the margin.

 This icon indicates a site that you access through a World Wide Web browser.

 This icon indicates a Usenet newsgroup, which you can read through any service that provides a newsreader.

 This icon indicates a mailing list, which you can receive through any e-mail service.

 This icon indicates a Gopher site, which is available through a Gopher service.

OTHER CONVENTIONS

Throughout the book, we have provided numerous suggestions about the Internet as well as about food and drink in general. Many of these will be identified as Notes, Tips, and Warnings.

A tip gives you some special bit of information that will help you in some way.

A note is some additional background information about the feature being discussed. It may clarify the operation or purpose of the feature.

Warnings provide information about some pitfalls—we have encountered all of them while researching this book—that you will want to avoid or some hidden costs.

This icon indicates the places we liked best.

Much of the Internet is under construction now and will continue to be. Some connections, because of their popularity or because they are located on a slow server, take time to load on your screen. If you are in a hurry, either stay away from these or be prepared to wait.

This icon indicates a site that we've included with some reservation.

WHAT TO DO ABOUT DISAPPEARING SITES

The addresses listed here are correct as of the book's printing. The Internet, however, is volatile. Addresses and locations are changing all the time—sites are moving to new and more powerful servers as more and more Internet users are connecting to them or current servers are reorganizing internally. When this happens, you do not always get change-of-address notices. If you get a message that one of the sites listed here does not exist, you have several options other than assuming the site has disappeared.

♦ It may be that you are trying to access a site that is temporarily down but that will be available later, in which case you can try again at another time.

♦ Perhaps you hit a traffic jam on the Information Superhighway, and things are so slow that they have come to a halt. If too many people try to access a site at one time, things get slower, and the last in line are refused access and have to try later. Perhaps another time of the day would be better.

♦ If an address has really changed, try one of the search tools discussed in the section of this book called *Finding Places on the Internet*, designed for just this purpose. Connect to one of these search tools, and enter some of the key words that appear in the site you want. You will be presented with a list of sites that you can access simply by clicking on them.

Part One:
The Basics

What Is the Internet?

As long as we have been using computers, we have been waiting for the perfect computer—the one that will have a cup of cappuccino and a croissant waiting for us when we wake up in the morning. Short of that, a lot of great stuff is available on your computer screen if you take the time to look around for it on the Internet. As the "net" part of the word indicates, the Internet is a *network*, but it is a *global* network consisting of a vast collection of interconnected computers.

Computer networks have become common in many of our lives, and you may be familiar with a Local Area Network (LAN), which is a group of computers connected to one another in the same building or over a short distance. A Wide Area Network (WAN) is a group of computers connected over a great distance. For example, a company that has branches in Chicago, Los Angeles, and London might connect all its computers with a WAN.

You can think of the Internet's structure in the same way you think of the telephone system, something we are all comfortable with that has been with us for quite a while. At one level, the phone system is an infrastructure of equipment. The web of trunk lines and telephone cables that connects all the switching stations and central exchanges exists to connect your telephone to all other phones in the system. In the same way, the infrastructure of the Internet provides a *backbone* (see Figure 1.1) that is comparable to a telephone trunk line. It provides the underlying structure of the system that allows all of us to be connected.

The Internet is similar to the phone system in another way. The Internet's sheer size and complexity involving thousands of interconnected computers always ensures an alternate route from one computer to another. When a connection is interrupted for some reason, the communication can take another path to its destination.

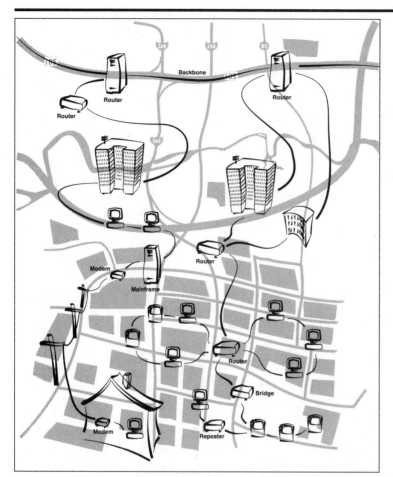

Figure 1.1:
The Internet
is like the
telephone
system,
connecting
individuals
with all other
available
locations.

And in yet another way, the phone system and the Internet are alike: Both are not merely cable, wire, and computer connections but people connections. The Internet is a community of computer users who come together in what is known as *cyberspace,* signaling a major change in the computer environment. During the 1960s and '70s the large and powerful (and expensive) *mainframe computers* predominated. Although the mainframe has less of a presence today, important to the Internet is a collection of very large and powerful computers, called *servers*, that can support many users and store large quantities of information. Servers are usually located at large government organizations and educational institutions that have an interest in maintaining public access. These computer servers act as large, central repositories of files that are publicly available to Internet users in much the same way that city and community libraries make books available to the public.

In the same way you use the phone system for a range of activities, so can you use the Internet for casual communication, business communication, advertising, research, and having fun.

 As you sit at your computer in your home or office, you may feel that your Internet communications are private. Not so. Be sure to use the Internet judiciously. If you are sending sensitive information or documents, do not assume that your information is protected until you have done research to assure yourself of the security level. Some software is specifically designed to provide security for protected interactions—financial or otherwise. You may want to use it.

WHO'S IN CHARGE HERE?

No one really knows the exact number of people who have used the Net since its inception, although estimates are that as many as 20 million people are currently accessing the Net and that the number is growing at something like 10 percent a month. But who is the president or CEO of this enterprise? Well, no single individual makes the final decisions. Groups such as the Internet Society (ISOC) and its subordinate group, the Internet Architecture Board, oversee the Internet from a technical standpoint. These people are volunteers who meet occasionally to determine the policies required to sustain the orderly growth of this thriving community.

Again like the telephone system, the Internet is a constantly changing, growing, organic entity. This entity is not a biological entity, of course, but exists because of the continual exchange of ideas and information. Through the Internet, all of us who use it are connected. Through it, as through the telephone system, we can communicate with one another in vastly expanded ways. Anyone who has access to a properly equipped personal computer and is connected to the Internet can exchange information in the form of text, images, sounds, animation, and video with anyone else connected to the Internet.

Most of the immediate daily operational decisions are made far from the policy-making organizations by the individual providers of Internet access services that seem to be springing up like fast-food restaurants throughout the country—and around the world. Your Internet service provider (ISP) gives you access to the Internet and determines the access level you will have to which services. The folks who work for the ISPs are similar to the regional telephone company employees who provide you local phone service. They

Some Historical Background

The Internet as we know it was spawned in the late 1960s by a group of Department of Defense scientists who wanted to share information among people working on similar research projects. The group, called the Advanced Research Projects Agency, began a project known as ARPAnet, which was designed to allow for rapid communication of large amounts of information. The project succeeded beyond the group's original expectations, and as word got out about the effectiveness of communicating electronically, the number of organizations wanting access to the network grew. Then, as the network expanded throughout the 1970s, members of the computer industry began to participate. By 1983, MILNET (the military network) split off from ARPAnet. Although the military organizations that compose MILNET maintain special security standards to safeguard themselves from hostile and malignant intrusions, e-mail gateways to MILNET are still maintained with the rest of the Internet.

Also at this time the TCP/IP (Transmission Control Protocol/Internet Protocol) was officially instituted on the Internet. Protocols are sets of rules that govern how information is sent from one computer to another and ensure that everyone can communicate. These rules, or standards, are maintained by the Internet Society. Still the predominant protocol on the Internet, TCP/IP establishes the rules by which files are broken into a series of discrete packets (a technical word for pieces) before being sent over the Internet. The packets of data, like letters within envelopes that also contain the destination and return addresses, travel separately. Packets are sent from server to server via the most efficient route. If one route is interrupted during a transmission because of something such as a power outage, the remaining packets can be sent again via any of the multitude of available routes that constitute the Internet and then can be reassembled at the destination.

will help you set up and help you resolve service problems. Daily these people are on the front lines of the rapidly expanding Internet.

Even so, already some groups and organizations are attempting to take hold of the Internet's reins. As the Internet's astonishingly robust growth continues, so probably will these attempts. Organizations such as the Federal Communications Commission (FCC) may try to place restrictions in response to issues that arise. For example, as of this writing, in one lawsuit an investment firm is trying to hold a major service provider responsible for statements posted by a subscriber. The subscriber's comments accuse the investment firm of criminal behavior. The investment firm insists that the service provider is responsible for monitoring the messages posted on its forums, while the service provider, of course, renounces any responsibility. To date, the Internet has been notoriously anarchic and unfettered by restrictions of any sort regarding the material made available to its users. Many users are staunchly committed to the idea of an environment in which the First Amendment is the predominant principle of law.

TESTING THE WATERS

A good way to start getting a feel for the cyberspace world is to subscribe to one of the commercial online service providers. The big three are CompuServe, America Online, and Prodigy. All three are discrete, self-contained services that offer a wide range of organized and closely monitored information about an expansive array of subjects, including numerous food topics from bread baking to wine vintages. Within each service, you can send and receive e-mail and browse the public discussion groups often called *forums*. In addition, you can venture outside each service to connect to the Internet to access newsgroups, to search the Internet for information, and to retrieve files containing information of interest to you.

The advantages of using an established commercial service are:

◆ A well-organized and documented set of menus in a clear format make it easy to find your way around.

◆ A secure environment ensures the integrity of files that you retrieve.

◆ A slick, sophisticated graphical interface (the display you see on the screen that presents choices through menus) is much more enticing than screens full of only text.

◆ A controlled framework offers a lot more hand holding and support than you will find in the free-form arenas on the Internet.

The disadvantages of using an established commercial service are:

◆ Extensive use can result in quickly mounting costs. Often it is possible to subscribe for a fixed fee (see *Costs of Internet Service Providers and Online Services* later in this chapter).

◆ A controlled environment means a confined one. And forays outside the parameters of a service, if your service even allows you to send e-mail and read newsgroup postings outside the service, can carry extra charges.

The commercial online services have been in business for quite a while—CompuServe was started in 1969 (see Figure 1.2). They provide well-managed, valuable services that are well worth investigating.

Figure 1.2:
CompuServe is the oldest of the three large online services.

 Well aware that more and more competitors are entering the arena every week, the services have made initial membership free and easy. Any time you purchase a new modem, new communications software, a new computer, or even a publication about online services, you will receive a coupon for a month of service at no cost. We even found an insert in a national computer magazine last month with that same offer for one month of free service.

What Can You Do on the Internet?

You are ready to see what the Internet has to offer, but where do you start? Trying to decide where to begin can be like having a $100 coupon for specialty food and wine at Trader Joe's, Fauchon's, or Zabar's. If you don't know the store, how would you begin? The Internet is a horn of plenty, and therefore its blessing is also its curse. Do you need to spend hours and hours online to find out what is there that you want, or is there a better, faster way to determine what is there and make some discriminating choices? When you tour California wine country's Napa Valley, you can taste and spit out your wine (as the professional tasters do) so as not to get drunk in the process of selecting your favorite Cabernet Sauvignon or Chardonnay. You can then buy a case to take home and enjoy at your leisure.

You can tour the Internet the same way. Described below are the most popular activities and the options they allow. You can go from one Internet location to another, be it Web pages or newsgroups, to browse the material at your leisure or to read the messages and respond to those that interest you. (See Figure 1.3.)

If you discover mailing lists that strike your fancy, subscribe to them at your leisure. The Internet offers an almost endless and constantly changing tour of a virtual Napa Valley. Numerous virtual tasting groups are already popping up on the Internet (see *Part Two*).

COMMUNICATE WITH E-MAIL

Perhaps the most universally attractive feature of online services is electronic mail, or e-mail (see Figure 1.4). More and more of us have computers on our desks much of the time, and what could be easier than using your computer to type a brief note of inquiry or greeting when the urge strikes.

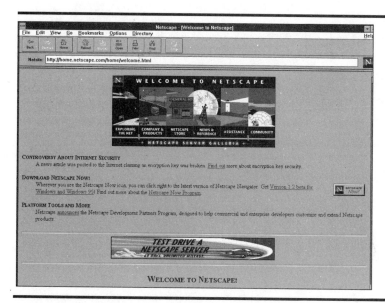

Figure 1.3:
You can view
Web pages with
one of the pop-
ular Web
browsers you
can get free on
the Internet.

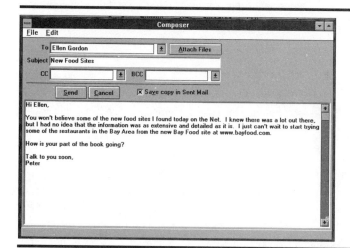

Figure 1.4:
Even Internet authors who
live in the same house use
e-mail.

E-mail works much the same as the good old reliable U.S. Mail—you compose the letter and send it when you want to and it arrives at the recipient's "mailbox" to be read whenever he or she wants. Unlike "snail mail" (a term for paper mail that is popular among computer users) however, e-mail can arrive at its destination in minutes or hours, depending on your service, no matter where the recipient is in the world. More and more of us have e-mail addresses. From our computers at home or at work, we can check the status of a message that we sent or look for a response whenever we want. No more waiting for the snail mail that arrives three days or more after it was sent.

All you need to know to communicate with someone who has access to the Internet is his or her e-mail address. This address takes the form of *username@domain*. The *username* is the name that every user must select when registering with a service. Our address, for example, is pstokes@hooked.net. The pstokes is a concatenation of *Peter Stokes*, and hooked.net is the name of the service to which we subscribe. *Hooked* is the name of the service, and *net* identifies the domain as a network administration (an organization similar to an ISP that provides access to and manages Internet connections for a group of people). The *domains* (a group of network host computers) you will most commonly see are identified in the Domain Name System (DNS). Here are the most familiar:

com	a commercial organization, business, or company
edu	an educational institution—some sort of school
int	an international organization
gov	a nonmilitary government entity
mil	a military organization
net	a network administration
org	other organizations: nonprofit, nonacademic, or nongovernmental

Indicative of the Internet's constant state of growth and change, some time in March 1995, the number of *com* sites exceeded the number of *edu* sites. This transition marks the evolution of the Net from its beginnings as a collection of educational and governmental organizations into a commercial entity. The National Science Foundation (NSF), once a central foundation of Internet support, has withdrawn NSFNet, and users who previously depended on it have gone to commercial ISPs. Does this mean the Net is shrinking? On the contrary, that independent providers can make viable commercial enterprises which offer Internet services attests to the Net's vigor.

E-Mail Addresses

Everyone who uses the Internet has a unique address, just as every U.S. citizen has a unique Social Security number. The *username@domain* convention can indicate not only the name of your service but also its location. For instance, doozer@tweazel.sf.ca.us indicates a username of doozer who is located at a service named tweazel in San Francisco, California, in the United States. The progression of the information in the address is hierarchical, from more specific to more general, just like the address on an envelope lists name, street address, city, state, and country. Here are some other international codes:

au	Australia
fr	France
de	Germany
it	Italy
uk	United Kingdom/Ireland

It's easy to correspond with someone who sends you a message. Most e-mail services let you "reply" to the messages you receive, in which case a message is returned to the original sender. When you receive a message from someone you might want to correspond with regularly, you can enter that person's e-mail address in your address list—a feature on most e-mail systems. After that, when you begin to compose a letter, you can simply choose that person's address from your automated address book.

Messages are transmitted on e-mail services as ASCII or text files. This is a plain vanilla kind of text file that contains no special formatting, fonts, or graphics and is limited to the characters your keyboard can put on the screen. Occasionally, the length of the message you can send is limited, but since the maximum size is 64,000 characters, this is not really a limitation in most cases.

If you are really inspired and find yourself exceeding this limit, simply cut your message into pieces. And, for example, label these pieces Part 1 of 5, Part 2 of 5, and so on. Be sure to tell the recipient what you have done so that he or she will know to assemble the parts into one message.

Another e-mail feature that you might find useful is the ability to send the same message simultaneously to multiple recipients. Handy for telling friends about a new wine you've just discovered or inviting several colleagues to a dinner party. Along with your message, you can include other files created on your computer system. For example, you can send a word-processing document of recipes or a spreadsheet of wine prices by attaching the file to your e-mail message.

Use caution when sending information to multiple recipients, especially if you are not sure of the reception. Unwanted sales pitches or unwelcome political positions can result in a hailstorm of antagonistic responses, known as flames.

SUBSCRIBE TO MAILING LISTS

A mailing list is no more than a collection of addresses linking people with common interests. Subscribing to a mailing list is similar to subscribing to a magazine or a journal that publishes information about areas of special interest to you. Just as you might subscribe to *Gourmet* to get recipes and cooking techniques and to *Sunset* for information about starting an herb garden or redesigning your kitchen, you can subscribe to any of thousands of Internet mailing lists in which people share information and opinions about every subject under the sun.

The difference between mailing lists and professionally published magazines is that many mailing lists are not edited or managed; that is, no one attends to the items being sent to all the subscribers. The possibilities for what you might receive are limitless. In addition, although you might look forward to receiving your beautifully designed issue of *Wine Spectator* full of lavish photos and elegant layouts, mailing lists come in the form of e-mail, which hasn't won many design awards recently.

When you subscribe to a mailing list, if you haven't had many correspondents previously, chances are you will have more than you ever thought possible. Be forewarned, if you are charged for the mail you receive on your service, you may rack up a substantial bill. Be sure to save the address of your mailing list as well as the instructions on how to unsubscribe (which you will receive along with the confirmation of your original subscription) so that you can shut off the flow if you find yourself inundated.

The method you'll use for subscribing depends on the kind of mailing list. The name of the list provides clues. Lists that begin with *listproc, listserv,* or *majordomo* are most probably managed by a computer program. For instance, a beer mailing list (no, it doesn't send out samples) has the name beer-l and the address listserv@ualvm.ua.edu. Subscribers to this list exchange beer-related information, experiences, and opinions. You can subscribe by sending e-mail to the address and the words "subscribe beer-l" followed by your name in the body of the message. If you are interested in subscribing to a *majordomo* list, such as that on *wines*, write the words "subscribe wines" in the body of your message and send it to majordomo@ee.pdx.edu. You need not include your name.

Don't add anything other than the required text to the message because the messages are being interpreted by computer programs. Perfectly reasonable requests stated in the wrong format will not be understood. Something such as "Please be so kind as to include me in the wines list. Thanks, Peter" would not be interpreted correctly.

CHECK OUT NEWSGROUPS

Newsgroups offer a focus that brings together diverse groups of people with shared interests to exchange information, just as mailing lists do. In a mailing list, a single message is sent to all subscribers, who may or may not respond. In a newsgroup, the message is posted in a public forum where individuals may or may not read it. Any responses to newsgroup messages are also posted in the public forum, to be read by subscribers at their whim.

Reading through the contents of a newsgroup in *Usenet* (the part of the Internet that contains newsgroups) is often a remarkable experience. Although many newsgroups are monitored, there is little censorship. Messages range from thoughtful, articulate responses to occasionally obscene attacks. Let him or her who posts a careless message beware—*newbies* (those new to the Internet and unfamiliar with the customs and practices) may be subject to unfriendly treatment.

The best way to see what is going on in the newsgroups is to lurk—to observe the postings and get a feel for the environment without making yourself known. You are not obligated to post a message if you find no reason. Later, when you've learned the customs, go ahead and participate. Most people who visit newsgroups are there to see what is going on anyway.

Newsgroups are a classic institution of the Internet. Anyone who feels so moved can post an opinion for the scrutiny of the rest of the world. When you feel the urge to contribute, go right ahead—that is what its all about. A truly impressive newsgroup that has remarkable scope is rec.food.cooking. This resource has a seemingly endless listing of recipes. Feel free to browse it when you need a recipe idea and your cookbooks at home don't seem to offer any inspirations.

You can subscribe to a newsgroup whenever you're in the mood, with no obligation or commitment. If you never get around to looking at what is on the group, nobody will be affected or offended. You can look to see what is there whenever you wish, and you can look to see the interchanges that are posted when you think you are interested in a subject. The posted articles are listed by a brief title, as shown in Figure 1.5.

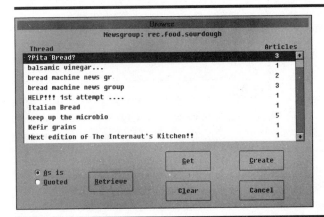

Figure 1.5:
A newsgroup listing of articles

If you decide you want to look at the article called "HELP!!! 1st attempt…," select that article. You'll find the message that's shown in Figure 1.6.

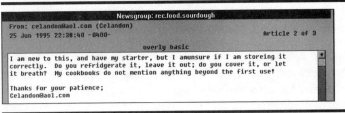

Figure 1.6:
A call for help—the meaning is clear even if the spelling isn't perfect.

Immediately following, a generous person sends along some information that responds to the call for help (see Figure 1.7).

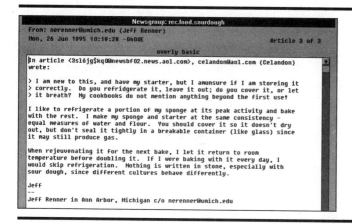

Figure 1.7:
A response to a newsgroup request

The response includes the message to which it is an answer so that anyone breaking in after the original message is gone can follow the discussion. Once you have read a message, it will be *scrolled off* the newsgroup for you and will not appear again. If you want to keep a particular message, you must save it on your own computer. Having done this, you can respond to it at your convenience. You can mail it as a private response to the sender's e-mail address, which is included in the original message. Or you can post it as an additional article in the *thread* (a string of articles that relate to the same topic) so that all who access the newsgroup can read it.

Anyone who has access to the Internet can post an article to a newsgroup. Therefore, discretion would argue against firing off an immediate angry response to someone who raises your ire. Thoughtfully worded and courteous responses will serve you best in every situation. Who knows who will be reading your submissions to this public forum and how they will be taken?

CONNECT WITH TELNET

You can connect to any one of hundreds of remote computers known as Telnet servers. These remote hosts, or Telnet *daemons* (autonomous software programs that operate in the background), are set up to allow you to run applications on them or to access their services, which are beyond the scope of your home computer. A service might be an index of recipes or a list of culinary equipment suppliers. When you connect to a Telnet host, it is as though your computer becomes a terminal that is directly connected to the larger machine and is accessing the service locally.

To make a Telnet connection, you need to know the name of the server and, if required, the login name and the password. Because the service is available to the public, the instructions are often displayed at the time of connection.

Detailed instructions about connecting via Telnet are beyond the scope of this book, but if you want to know more, see Sybex's *The Internet Roadmap* by Bennet Falk, an excellent detailed reference on the services available over the Internet.

BRINGING HOME THE BACON WITH FTP

File Transfer Protocol (FTP) is an excellent tool for retrieving files from the numerous remote public sites on the Internet. Using FTP, you can enter a remote site, usually a server, and view the contents of the public directories. FTP servers are established precisely for the purpose of making files available to whomever wants to use them. After viewing the files available in the public directories, you can copy any of them to your own computer. Because this application does not require an individual account or a login on the server, it is known as *anonymous FTP.*

To use an FTP server, simply enter the address of the remote computer (Site Name) and the login name (User Name) *anonymous*, as shown in Figure 1.8.

If you are required to enter additional information, such as your e-mail address in the place of a password, you will be instructed about what to do (see Figure 1.9).

You are free to browse through the directory structure of the remote computer (see Figure 1.10) to choose the files you want to *download* (copy from a remote host or server to your own computer).

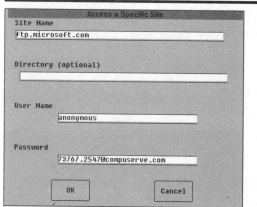

Figure 1.8:
Connecting to an FTP site at Microsoft

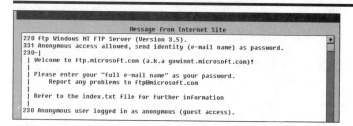

Figure 1.9:
Instructions from an
FTP connection

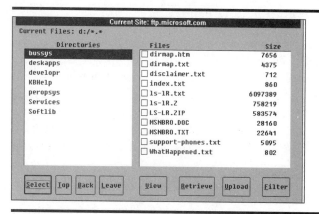

Figure 1.10:
Directories at the Microsoft
FTP site

Downloading Compressed Files

Files at FTP sites are frequently compressed, or made smaller, with utility software. When files are compressed, they take up less disk space, and login time on the server is decreased. They transfer faster, and you save money if you are paying for service by the hour. The trade-off is that you must decompress the file after it is downloaded.

On PCs a popular compression format is ZIP, which is created by a utility program called PKZIP. You can recognize a zipped file by the extension in the file name (the part of the file name that follows the period). A zipped file is named FILENAME.ZIP. When you decompress zipped files, you UNZIP them.

If you have a Mac, you won't want to be without Stuffit Expander, which decompresses files. A file that has been compressed with Stuffit has the extension SIT in the file name.

Some files are self-extracting. A self-extracting file is one that has been compressed for quicker transmission over the network; it can restore itself to full size without any special utility program. On the Mac, these files are identified by an SEA (self-extracting archive) extension. On the PC, a self-extracting file has an EXE extension. Keep in mind that the EXE extension appears in many executable files, so it is not a unique identifier of self-extracting files.

GO SHOP AROUND ON THE NET

So here you go, ready to charge out into the great wide world of the Internet. But where will you head? You need to pick up something to eat, but unless you have an idea about what kind of store you want to patronize—a delicatessen, a pizza parlor, or a supermarket—how are you going to decide which direction to go? A number of Internet tools can help you find your way around. Fortunately, you don't need to know the exact name and location of every file and every page you want. One of the great tools is known as *Gopher* (as in "It's almost dinner time. Why don't you go-pher some pizza and beer?"). Gopher is an application developed at the University of Minnesota and named for the school mascot. Gopher is menu based, and with it a user who has the proper software installed can locate files on any of the numerous Gopher servers on the Internet. The advantage of using Gopher is that you need not know the location of the file you want before you begin. If your file is on any Gopher server anywhere, the search will be conducted and the file located without any direction from you. If you see a URL (an abbreviation for Universal Resource Locator—the Internet address of a document on an Internet server) that begins with *gopher,* you know immediately that it points to a location on a Gopher server. The Gopher FAQ (an acronym for a document that contains Frequently Asked Questions and their answers), for instance, can be found at gopher://mudhoney.micro.umn.edu:70/00/Gopher.FAQ (shown in Figure 1.11).

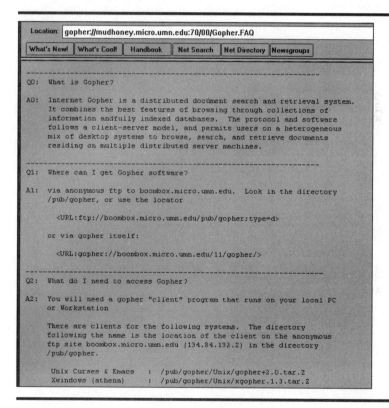

Figure 1.11:
The Gopher FAQ

Another helpful Internet tool is the *Wide Area Information Service* (WAIS). As does Gopher, WAIS shields you from having to know the location or even the specific name of the file for which you are searching. WAIS depends on an indexing system. The text of a document must be indexed by someone for it to be available in a WAIS search.

Yahoo is another search and reference tool, specific to the *World Wide Web (WWW)*. The World Wide Web is made up of all the documents at computer sites that are connected—linked—by the existence of the Internet. Yahoo is available only with a Web *browser* (software that allows users to move around the World Wide Web and interact with Web documents); it is a list of Internet locations and resources (see Figure 1.12). Originally developed by Stanford University students, Yahoo has become an independent service that provides an excellent starting point for getting an idea of what's out there.

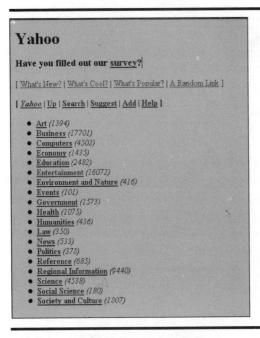

Figure 1.12:
Yahoo will serve as the beginning of many of your World Wide Web searches.

You can see that the range is fairly universal here, and that is the idea. The list is inclusive—not focused in any way, so it is a resource that is hard to use up. Take a look at the listings in Yahoo's Food and Eating site found at http://www.yahoo.com/Entertainment/Food (see Figure 1.13).

As you can see, Yahoo contains listings for all kinds of resources, including commercial establishments.

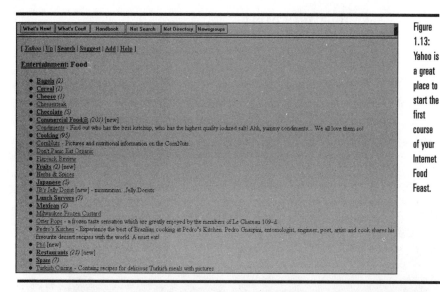

Figure 1.13: Yahoo is a great place to start the first course of your Internet Food Feast.

Finding Places on the Internet

The number of search resources on the Internet is increasing all the time. Here is a sample of some other services that can help you find your way around, many of which, largely for commercial sites, are organized like the Yellow Pages.

Resource	URL (Internet address)	What you will find here
Web Crawler	http://webcrawler.com/	A free search resource operated by America Online
Infoseek	http://www.infoseek.com	Automated, business-oriented index; commercial service with a limited free search utility
Lycos	http://www.lycos.com/	Carnegie Mellon search utility
World Wide Web Worm	http://www.cs.colorado.edu/home/mcbryan/WWWW.htm	
IISP Yellow Pages	http://www.index.org	Index of businesses on the World Wide Web
YellowPages	http://theyellowpages.com	Exhaustive listing with many links

BROWSE WEB PAGES

In a sense, the most complete realization of the Internet is the World Wide Web (WWW). In Net lingo, when you browse the net, you *surf* it. Thus, you need a *surfboard*. Your Net surfboard consists of a computer configured with the hardware and the software that we discuss in the following sections (see Figure 1.14). You can move around the globe from one Web location to another, never leaving your chair. Arriving at the Web sites you choose, you will be treated to marvelous graphics, audio, and even video with which you can interact if you have adequate hardware and software.

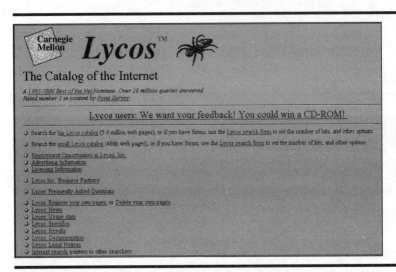

Figure 1.14: Lycos is one of the very useful search tools for finding you way around the Internet's World Wide Web.

The Web was developed in the early 1990s at the European Center for Nuclear Research (The *Conseil Europeen pour la Recherche Nuclearie,* or CERN) as an environment in which scientists in Geneva, Switzerland, could share research information. It has evolved into a medium in which users can create multimedia documents containing text, graphics, audio, and even video.

The term *Web* is actually a metaphor for the way all elements of the World Wide Web are connected. Any of us who has become accustomed to moving around from file to file in a computer has had to learn something about the hierarchical structure of the way data is stored. Being logical creatures, computers function most effectively when files are categorized in directories that allow them to store and retrieve information more easily. When you go to a grocery store to buy milk, you ask where the dairy section is, and once you get there, you begin to look for the specific type and size of milk you want. If things were stored randomly or if new items were put in the next available shelf space, imagine what it would be like to find anything in a large grocery store. Whether you use a Macintosh that puts files in *folders* or a PC that uses DOS *directories* or graphical windows to differentiate file types, you have become accustomed to finding the category that contains the file or document you seek and then searching around within that area for the file itself. On the Internet, you go through such a process when you traverse FTP directories, for example.

In menu-based, hierarchical computer systems, we move from place to place through stairstep sequences of files and directories. On the Web, we move from place to place directly. The user becomes, if you will, a spider able to move from point to point at his or her will. This feat is accomplished by the technological marvel of *hypertext*.

WHAT IS HYPERTEXT?

Hypertext, a term attributed to Ted Nelson of the Xanadu project, describes terms that provide immediate links to other documents. The links might explain or give background information on the original word, and this additional information can be presented in graphical, audio, or video form as well as text. Imagine learning a foreign language by reading a document that, when you clicked on any word, would pronounce the word and provide the meaning in your native language.

To construct a document of this sort, you create the links with the *Hypertext Markup Language* (HTML), a labor-intensive undertaking. Figure 1.15 is an example of the HTML code that lies behind the Virtual Vineyards page that follows (see Figure 1.16).

The highlighted, underlined words in the text identify the links. Simply clicking on them takes you to another document or location.

To move to one of the locations, for example, to Featured Wineries, simply move the cursor to the highlighted, underlined text Featured Wineries. When you do this, the cursor changes from an arrow to a hand, and on your screen appears a Web page displaying Featured Wineries, as promised (see Figure 1.17).

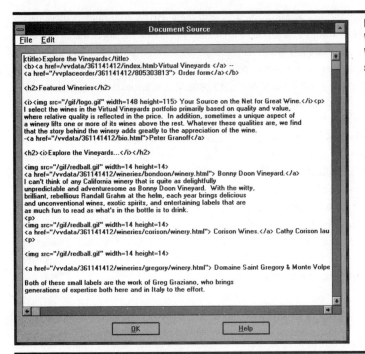

Figure 1.15:
What lies underneath a
Web page—an HTML
source document

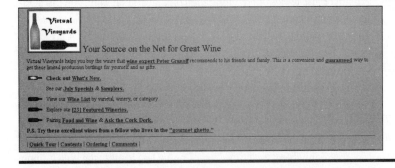

Figure 1.16:
The Virtual
Vineyards
Web page as
it appears on
the Net

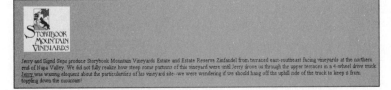

Figure 1.17:
Click on a
link and find
yourself
transported
to Storybook
Vineyards.

These links contain *URLs,* which are the addresses to Web pages. The URL to Virtual Vineyards is http://www.virtualvin.com. By clicking on a link that interests you, your online session is moved to the URL that lies under the highlighted, underlined text. It is easy to find yourself connected to a computer in some remote part of the world, investigating a cuisine that you never even imagined.

Getting Online

Our first online experience was connecting to a banking service during the mid 1980s using a Leading Edge computer, one of the early IBM clones and our first PC. It was hot stuff then. What a thrill it was to be able to connect to the bank at any time during the day or night to be able to check balances, pay bills, or transfer money from one account to another. The monochrome monitor we used at the time was just fine for the *interface* (the screen display you see during your online session generated by the communication software your service provides), especially since that interface was *character based*—it only used words, no images or colors. That computer would still be fine today for the online service to the bank and for many computer bulletin boards.

Even more exciting was signing up for an online service and exchanging e-mail with a relative who was living overseas at the time. You can still access character-based bulletin boards and e-mail services using a monochrome monitor, and probably even with decade-old equipment, but newer equipment that provides a more attractive graphical interface has certainly made our online lives more pleasant and colorful. You don't have to invest a small fortune in equipment to connect to the online world, but you do need some basic standards to access the exciting services that are now available. Upgrading your hardware is comparable to what we did when we had our kitchen remodeled: We replaced our thrift store Wedgewood stove with a contemporary stove/broiler that has digital controls and electronic ignition. We could have continued with the Wedgewood, but our added pleasure in cooking and baking has more than justified the cost.

Let's look at what's needed in the way of hardware.

YOUR COMPUTER AND MODEM

At the basic level, you need a computer and a modem to access the Internet, and you have a wide range of choices. The purpose of this section is not to recommend specific brands or companies, but to provide some guidelines for making decisions about the minimum levels of equipment you need.

If you were to ask, What is the best wine to go with a spicy, complex dish such as curry? we would suggest you get an appropriate variety of wine *in a price range you can afford*. In the same way, we would not suggest that everyone rush out and purchase the fastest, most powerful, most expensive Pentium computer available for the purpose of connecting to the Internet. Your current equipment may very well be just fine. It may also be that a moderate upgrade would be in order. Also, the bank balance is always a primary consideration in our house.

Either a PC or a Macintosh (we are using both to write this book) will serve your purposes. What you want, to take advantage of the great graphics on the Internet, is a color monitor. Although monitors have held their prices most tenaciously of all computer components, they have finally begun to decline, and you can get quite an acceptable monitor for about $200.

 Take your time to look around for used equipment if you don't have to make your purchase immediately. The market is loaded with equipment that is perfectly good, but no longer "cutting edge." If you feel uncertain about buying used equipment, consult a knowledgeable friend or find a computer store that will evaluate components for you and provide support if you need it.

As much as you can afford to, invest your equipment money in processor speed and the size of your fixed disk, or hard drive (where your files are stored). Speed is derived from many components, but the basic is your CPU, or *central processing unit*. This is the brain of your computer, and the place where most of the work gets done. You may have a 386, a 486, or a Pentium computer. These designations indicate the power of the CPU that is driving your machine. Of these three types, the Pentium is the most powerful, then the 486, and then the 386. The more powerful the CPU, the faster you can move from one task to another, and the less time you will spend waiting for tasks to complete.

The CPU is the head chef of the kitchen, but all chefs depend on a number of assistants. For example, RAM, or *random access memory,* is another major contributor to the efficiency of your computer's performance. Without enough RAM, you will spend a lot of your online time waiting for processes to complete. If you have fewer than 8 megabytes (8MB) of RAM, you should consider adding more. You will be amazed at the difference.

A less crucial but still significant factor is the amount of storage space on your computer's hard drive. If you don't have enough free space, you won't be able to download the files and programs that are available to all users on the Internet. We would have a hard time justifying the purchase of a drive that can hold fewer than 200MB of data. If you are in the market for a new machine, look for something in the area of 500MB if you can afford it. You can never have too much disk space. It's like a pantry that seems to fill itself up spontaneously.

SELECTING A MODEM

Another important participant in your Internet experience is your modem.

Modems come in both *internal* and *external* versions: an internal modem fits into a slot inside your computer's case, and an external modem plugs into a *port* (a connection on the back of your computer). The modem mediates between your computer and other computers, and to be able to contact other computers, it must also be plugged into a telephone jack.

The speed at which you transfer data—files and images—back and forth over the Internet depends on the speed at which your modem operates. The speed of modems is expressed in *bits per second* (bps), which is also referred to as the baud rate and which indicates how fast data moves to and from your computer. At this writing, the current standard, which is available on all the national online services and supported by most local

Communications Basics

Modem is one of those jargon words that identifies an essential element for connecting to the Internet. A concatenation of the words modulate and demodulate, the word *modem* identifies a device that allows your computer to communicate with other computers over a telephone line. Computers talk to each other using digital signals, which are different from the analog signals transmitted over most telephone cables. The modem translates the messages you generate with your computer into the kind of signals that can be sent over the phone lines that run into your home. Another modem on the other end of the line receives the analog signal and converts it back to a digital format that the computer on the other end can understand.

providers, is 14,400 bps, sometimes referred to as 14.4K bps. Quickly approaching is the next standard, however, which is 28,800 bps, so if you are considering investing in a new modem, we would advise purchasing a 28.8K bps model. If you have a 9,600 bps modem, you can certainly access whatever you wish, but you may not be so happy with the amount of time you have to wait for processes to complete online. You can even perform online functions at less than 9,600 bps. At 1,200 bps, a modem performs basic functions such as sending and reading e-mail or browsing newsgroups, but to access the myriad great graphics and to run the software that is currently available, you need equipment that will perform at a higher speed.

DEDICATED PHONE LINES

A brief note about establishing a phone line to use for your Internet connection: Although it is not necessary to install an additional phone line solely for the purpose of accessing online services, you might want to consider a few of the implications. If you have only one phone line that you use as a voice line (the one you use to make telephone calls), you can certainly use it to connect with the Internet. Radio Shack and other electronic stores sell inexpensive plastic devices that allows you to attach two or even three phones to one phone jack (see Figure 1.18).

Figure 1.18:
An easy way to make two phone jacks out of one

Although you can attach the devices to one line, you can use only one device at a time. While you are connected to your favorite newsgroup checking out the most recent responses to the articles that have been posted, anyone who tries to call you will receive a busy signal. Solutions to this problem range from signing up for an answering service (or voice mail if it's available in your area) that will accept messages for you while your line is busy to acquiring another line for your home. We were surprised at the modest cost of a second phone line that is used only for computer connections. Although costs vary by region and your local phone company may charge more or less, you'll probably pay about $10 a month for basic service and less than $100 for installation. In addition, you can use this line for a fax machine, which we do, allowing our voice line always to be available for incoming and outgoing telephone calls. We can spend as much time online as necessary without worrying about missing incoming calls.

INTERNET SERVICES

After selecting and setting up your hardware, you are only at the beginning of the process of getting connected. The next step is to select an Internet service provider.

INTERNET SERVICE THROUGH COMMERCIAL ONLINE SERVICES

As discussed previously (see *Testing the Waters* earlier in this section), one way of doing this is to sign up with one of the three large commercial providers: CompuServe, America Online, or Prodigy. Another addition to this group is Microsoft's online service, which is included with every copy of Windows 95, guaranteed to become the predominant operating system. All these services offer a controlled environment with a number of basic services, available for a monthly fee, and other special or premium services for additional hourly rates. We subscribe to several of these services for their dependability and to access the many technical support services available there.

Online Services v. the Internet

For years, long before widespread public access to the Internet was a possibility, the commercial online services offered a number of proprietary services that are accessible only to members of the service. These "in-house" services are different and apart from the newsgroups, mailing lists, and e-mail available on the Internet. To access the Internet from one of these services, you will pay an additional hourly charge above and beyond the monthly membership fee. It may be that you find much of value on these services, but they constitute a separate, parallel branch to Internet services.

INTERNET SERVICE THROUGH NATIONAL AND LOCAL SERVICE PROVIDERS

Increasingly, you can access through the Internet the online support services that were previously available only on CompuServe, America Online, or Prodigy. Many software and hardware companies provide Web pages that feature support forums, so it is no longer necessary to join a national online service to communicate with these companies.

Particularly if you live in a major metropolitan area, you can access the Internet through a local service provider. The advantages of doing business with a local service provider are the same as the advantages of doing business with any local merchant. Technical assistance close to you deals with any problems. If you have ever had to get something repaired through a mail-order company, you know what we're talking about. Chances are, the costs of local service will be equal to or better than the cost of a commercial provider. Many times, local providers are able to offer good prices by supplying a *shell account* (a Unix-based Internet access in which you type characters rather than clicking on pictures with a mouse). Although shell accounts have been traditionally associated with older Unix systems that did not support the graphics of the current Internet, it is possible, with some degree of effort, to use an emulation program called TIA (The Internet Adapter), a *shareware* program that will allow you to use a shell account to run a graphical Web browser. Shareware is software that you can obtain and try for free, but are asked to pay a modest sum for if you elect to use it. Although setup involves extra steps, it is possible to get the same functionality from a shell account as you do from a more expensive SLIP (Serial Line Internet Protocol) or PPP (Point-to-Point Protocol) account. Setting up a shell account for the first time requires extra effort, but that effort pays off in smaller monthly charges in the long run.

If you have to make a toll call to access your provider, that alone is reason to switch to a service you can access with a local call. If you want to have more control over the software interface through which you experience the Internet, that is another reason to consider a local provider. Local providers may allow you more leeway with your Net connection.

When you are considering signing up for an account with a local service provider, be sure to find out the range of services they provide and what your startup as well as your initial costs will be.

A List of Questions for Your Potential Service Provider

♦ Is there a setup fee? If so, how much is it and what comes with it?

♦ What are the plan options (flat monthly rate, hourly charges)?

♦ Is the service available via a local call?

♦ What kind of connection is offered—SLIP, PPP, or shell account? Must you use a proprietary interface to connect to the service?

♦ If not, can you use whatever software you wish?

If you have some choices in your area about which services to use, call them all and ask each the same questions so that you can find the best deal. The market is highly competitive and rapidly expanding, so take advantage of the new companies out there and their eagerness to please.

SEEING IS BELIEVING: WEB BROWSERS

Once you get an ISP, the next step is to set up your software. Many providers offer their own software to aid you in connecting to and using e-mail and newsgroups and sometimes even in browsing Web sites. If you do not receive software when you sign up with your ISP, excellent resources are available to help you get started (see Sybex's *Mosaic Access to the Internet,* by Daniel A. Tauber and Brenda Kienan or *The Mosaic Roadmap,* by Robin Merrin, both of which go into the installation and use of Web browsers). There is a wealth of public domain (free) software and shareware.

A remarkable software program, NCSA Mosaic, is available to the public at no charge. This excellent Web browser was the original Mosaic, developed by the National Center for Supercomputing Applications at the University of Illinois, and continues to be enhanced and refined. To use it, you must have already made a substantial investment in computer hardware and other software, but once you are set up, you can download and install this program on your computer.

Costs of Internet Service Providers and Online Services

We have heard some express the notion that the Internet is somehow a free service. This is a great misconception. Even if you belong to an organization that allows you free access to the Internet, *someone* is paying for the computer equipment you are using for your online sessions, as well as providing the phone lines over which you are connecting. Most of us are able to use the Internet because we pay monthly fees for the services that provide us access to the Net. Here are a range of options for comparison's sake. Select the provider that suits your needs best. As discussed earlier, the commercial online services provide their own proprietary offerings in addition to varying degrees of Internet access.

Table 1.1: Rates of Internet Service Providers and Online Services

Provider	Monthly Rate	Hourly Rate	Startup Fee
America Online	$9.95 (includes 5 hours of Internet connect time)	10 cents/minute after the first 2 hours	None
CompuServe	$9.95 (includes 5 hours of Internet connect time)	$2.95/hour after the first 5 hours	None
CompuServe Internet Club	$24.95 (includes 20 hours of Internet connect time)	$1.95/hour after 20 hours	None
CRL (basic shell account)	$17.50 (unlimited Internet connect time)	None	$19.50
Delphi	$10 (4 hours) or $20 (20 hours) + $3/month for Internet access	$19 for the $10 plan or $9 for the $20 plan	3 cents/minute after your allowed hours
Netcom	$19.50	None	$25
Prodigy	$9.95 (includes 5 hours of Internet connect time)	25 cents/minute	None
Microsoft Network	$4.95 (includes 3 hours)	$2.50/hour	None

Customs and Manners

Part of a good upbringing used to consist of instruction in the standards of politeness and manners espoused by Emily Post in her famous book *Etiquette*. From it you could find out how to set the table for a formal dinner party, how soon to send out the invitations, and when to use paper or cloth napkins. Although that book no longer enjoys its former authority, many of its standards live on in the standards of conduct by which many people live today. Although the culture of the Internet is too new and too volatile to codify in such a manner, we can offer a number of reasonable suggestions to help you know what to expect at this digital feast. *Netiquette*, or the etiquette of the Internet, is not something to be taken lightly.

WHAT'S EXPECTED OF NEWBIES

If you are new to the Internet, you are what is known as a newbie. Although there is considerable discussion about newbies and their transgressions, we cannot remember even one incident in which a newbie was ridden out of town on a rail or tarred and feathered. Although you may be new to the experience, if you conduct yourself in reasonable ways, you will be treated like anyone else. See if you can identify the behavior that characterizes appropriateness; if you don't know, *ask questions*. Asking questions is a perfectly legitimate use of the Internet. Of course, there are automated tools that will help you find your way around (see *Finding Places on the Internet*, above), but automated tools can't answer questions the same way that humans can—at least not yet. For instance, if you were posting a question in the alt.food.ice-cream newsgroup about dessert recipes to serve for your Internet user group dinner, you might be directed to the alt.food.chocolate newsgroup to see the discussion of the perfect double-fudge iced dessert. People are more than willing to help kindred spirits they find on the Net.

Use the same kind of common sense that you would use in any sort of communications with others. Express yourself as clearly and concisely as possible. Too much is out there to look at for people to spend time wading through rambling, repetitive, vague expression. Write with politeness and respect, even when disagreeing with or correcting others. Hostile attacks are not interesting or attractive to others and will not stand you in good stead if the wrong person reads them. Remember, the Internet is a *global* network, and people from everywhere have access to what is posted there. Many of these ideas apply to e-mail as well. Of course, e-mail is by nature a more intimate medium in which your message will not be exposed to the scrutiny of a global audience, but once the message has left your computer, it is out of your hands and cannot be retrieved for alteration.

Watch your peas and queues out there. Like blatant advertising and gross factual errors, egregious spelling errors and careless typos are sometimes subject to surprisingly harsh criticism. A lot of English majors are out there, and many of them have computers. One way of protecting yourself without hiring an editor is to use a word processor and run your message through a spelling check before you send it.

WHEN IN ROME

When you are first getting acquainted with a newsgroup or a mailing list, spend some time learning what it is like. What is the range of subjects? What tone of conversation predominates? If you are dialing in to a wine newsgroup to exchange impressions of vintages of Nuits-Saint Georges (French Burgundy made from Pinot Noir grapes) and all you can find is messages about White Zinfandel and wine coolers, you might get the impression that you have landed in the wrong place. You might, in that case, try alt.bacchus or alt.food.wine to see if the general level of discussion matches yours.

Get the FAQs. One of the first places to go in any newsgroup is to the FAQ (Frequently Asked Questions) listing for some general information about what sort of dishes are generally served up. The FAQ for the Vegan-L mailing list (see Figure 1.19) is a statement of philosophy as well as information about what goes on in the mailing list.

The same sort of information that appears in an FAQ may be found in postings with names such as news.announce.newusers. You can find out whether

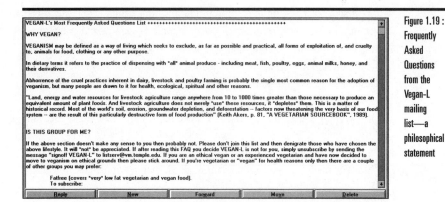

Figure 1.19 : Frequently Asked Questions from the Vegan-L mailing list—a philosophical statement

the newsgroup is set up as a discussion group or as a place for announcements and information requests or in some other format. Just as when you visit a foreign country, you are in a much better position having informed yourself about the customs before you arrive. If you go into a Russian restaurant and request chopsticks, you will be met with blank stares.

Lurk Before You Leap. This initial period in which you are investigating a newsgroup and its environs before contributing is called lurking. You have a chance to observe the kinds of reactions received by those who post articles. You can see that some Usenet users do not take kindly to having their time taken up with messages that are not of public interest. If you post a query searching for recipes using green tomatoes in the fall when your tomato plants are dying in the frosts and some kind person gives you a recipe for green tomato chutney, don't post an article in public thanking that person. Use e-mail in private to send that thanks directly. You will notice that at the top of each posting the e-mail address of the sender (that is, the return address) is listed, and you can use that to communicate directly with the individual. The Internet may seem unlimited, but at the current rate of growth, there is no need to post a personal thank-you note for thousands to read.

Don't Be the Headline Horseman. Some users don't seem able to resist the desire to post messages that are generally available in the newspaper headlines. Headline postings are more of a problem in newsgroups that are oriented toward announcements and events, such as sports newsgroups. For example, if you read a front-page article about a freeze in Brazil that is expected to raise global coffee prices, there is no need to post an article that summarizes the newspaper story. Your fellow caffeine consumers will probably be out at the store stocking up on French-roast beans while you are writing a posting about something they already know. Along the same lines, there is no need to make parallel postings in similar newsgroups, which is called *spamming*. Folks who frequent the net will most likely be aware of newsgroups on the same subject.

Other Assorted Gaffes to Avoid. Don't put up "Test" postings—7 million potential readers don't want to download your empty test messages. Advertisements are not received well in newsgroups or mailing lists; other forums are available for commercial enterprise, and newsgroup readers seldom take kindly to solicitation. As clever as they can be, excessive *signatures* (the four-line attachments at the end of many Internet postings that contain additional information about the sender) are unnecessary expressions of self-aggrandizement. Some netizens even frown on the designs created from text characters that some people include with their postings (see Figure 1.20).

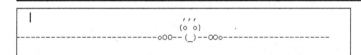

Figure 1.20:
The art of the keyboard

Internet Idioms

A manifestation of the desire for fun particular to newsgroups is what's known as emoticons or smileys. You may or may not care for these outgrowths of the keyboard culture, but they are here to stay, perhaps as expressions of the irrepressible sense of fun that runs throughout the Internet. If at first you don't quite get it, turn your head sideways and look.

   :-)   A happy smiley

   8-)   A smiley wearing glasses

   ;-)   A winking smiley

:-(A sad smiley

:-x   A kissing smiley

:^)   A smiley looking up at the sky

%-)   A disoriented (crazy) smiley

8°   An astonished smiley

<g>   Smiley's first cousin—a grin

As you will see, the possibilities are endless. Either lots of folks out there have active imaginations, or they don't have much to keep them busy.

After all the dire warnings and cautionary suggestions, newsgroups are mostly fun as well as interesting, and people like to have a good time with newsgroup articles within their contexts.

Another favorite of newsgroup users is the acronym—again a function of being tied to the keyboard. Any strategy that can save some typing is valuable. This genre is open for creativity too, but be careful about what you use if you want your recipient to understand you.

BTW	By the way
FCOL	For crying out loud
FYI	For your information
IMO	In my opinion
IMHO	In my humble opinion
LOL	Laughing out loud
OTOH	On the other hand
ROTFL	Rolling on the floor laughing
RTM/RTFM	Read the manual!/Read the @%$*!!&ing manual
TAFN	That's all for now

Internet and Gourmet Lingo

Like tasting wine, brewing beer, baking bread, or preparing sushi, traveling the Internet involves an abundance of specialized terminology peculiar to the culture. Here is a list of many of the most common terms you will encounter as you get to know the Internet.

al dente	pasta cooked with just the right amount of chewiness—literally "to the tooth"
anonymous FTP	the File Transfer Protocol that allows anyone, without a special password or a login name, to connect to and download from designated Internet servers
BBS	bulletin board system; a computerized bulletin board you can connect to using a modem
botrytis	a mold (known as noble rot in France) that attacks grapes under the right conditions, causing them to lose moisture, acidity, and gain sugar content. Wines made from these grapes are smooth, have a soft blend of honey and fruit flavors, and are most often served as dessert wines.
bouquet	the scent of wine that is produced by evaporation; the first perfume of a wine is the bouquet—the longer, more lingering odor is the aroma.
client	an individual computer that connects to a server. *See* server.
compressed	a file that is compacted, or made smaller, by a software utility program. Because it takes up less space, it can be transmitted faster.
convection oven	an oven that has an internal fan so that the heat is more evenly distributed; food is cooked more evenly and more quickly.
cyberspace	the online culture that the Internet creates

daemon	an autonomous software program operating in the background that allows you to run applications or to access the services of remote computers
double creme/triple creme	French terms used to classify cheese by the amount of butterfat they contain: 60% butterfat is double creme, and 70% butterfat is triple creme.
download	transfer a file from a remote computer, usually a server, to your local computer. *See* upload.
en croute	food that is wrapped and baked in a light, buttery pastry crust; this can range from cheeses (Brie en croute) to meats (beef Wellington).
espresso/cappuccino	finely ground, dark-roasted coffee made by forcing hot water through the grinds under great pressure; cappuccino is espresso served with frothy, steamed milk. Neither is for the faint of heart.
flame	a derisive, possibly insulting message posted on a newsgroup or mailing list
e-mail	electronic mail; the popular service by which computer users communicate with one another on a computer network
Farmhouse cheese	traditional British cheese made on individual farms throughout the countryside. Farmhouse cheeses possess rich, distinctive flavors.
FTP	File Transfer Protocol; a method of moving files between two computers.
GIF	an abbreviation for Graphics Interchange Format, a format for graphics files
hot list	a list of your favorite Internet sites stored in your Web browser program for convenient access
HTML	an abbreviation for Hypertext Markup Language, the language used to create World Wide Web documents from ordinary text
hyperlink	a highlighted word, phrase, or image in a Web document that contains a connection to another part of the current document, a different document, or even a document in a different computer
hypertext	on a Web page, underlined and/or highlighted text that contains links to other Internet documents or locations

lurk to visit a newsgroup and spend time reading the entries without creating any entries of your own or responding to any of those that you read; an advisable strategy for newbies. *See* newbie.

mailing list a list of e-mail addresses, sometimes maintained by a moderator, that receive messages sent out in relation to a particular subject area

Mosaic any one of several programs that allow you to browse World Wide Web pages, taking advantage of the hyper-text links

newbie a new computer user who is still learning the ropes

Netscape a Web-browser program, much like Mosaic, that allows you to locate and view hypertext documents

packet a discrete container of data, like a letter in an envelope, with an address and contents, that contains a portion of a file being sent over a network. When all the packets arrive at their destination, they are reassembled into a complete file.

protocol a set of common rules that allow transactions to occur

PPP an abreviation for Point-to-Point Protocol; one of many standards that allow computers to communicate across a remote connection

search engine any one of numerous programs available on the Internet to search various Internet databases for locations containing references to a subject of interest to you

sediment the solid matter that settles to the bottom of the bottle of certain wines (particularly rich red wines) over time; wine with significant sediment in it should be decanted to avoid a cloudy appearance.

self-extracting a file that is compressed for faster transmission and that will expand itself automatically. Its filename contains an EXE extension.

server a computer, usually fairly large, that can be used to allow client computers access to information such as a BBS or an Internet service. *See* client.

shareware software programs that you can use for a limited time for no cost. If you like the program and want to continue using it after the initial trial period, you pay the creator of the program and often receive information about future upgrades and/or documentation. These programs are usually quite inexpensive.

shell account	an Internet service account based on the Unix operating system. You must know Unix commands to navigate the Internet with a shell account.
SLIP	an abbreviation for Serial Line Internet Protocol—one of many standards that allow computers to communicate across a remote connection
sparkling wines	wines made by adding carbonation to the fermentation process. In France these wines are called Champagne; in Italy, Spumante; and in the U.S., sparkling wine.
standard	a formally agreed-upon set of rules or measurements for computer hardware, software, and communication devices that determines performance level. For example, a 14.4K bits per second (bps) modem transmits data at 14,400 bits per second.
surfing	moving around from one site to another on the Internet, using the hypertext links that are available on Web pages
TCP/IP	an abbreviation for Transmission Control Protocol/Internet Protocol; the communications standards on which the Internet is based
thread	a series of messages in a newsgroup consisting of the original and the responses to it
Telnet	a program that allows a computer to connect to a remote system and run programs on that system
TIA	an abbreviation for The Internet Adapter, a shareware program that enables you to use a less expensive shell account to access the World Wide Web in all its graphical glory
tisane	fresh herbs or tea leaves steeped in hot water; a more delicate flavor than dried tea leaves
TIF	an acronym for Tagged Image File, a format for graphics files
upload	to transfer a file from your home computer to a network server or a bulletin board. *See* download.
URL	an abbreviation for Uniform Resource Locator, the address of a place—a service or a Web page—on the Internet
Vegan	vegetarians who eat neither meat, dairy products, or eggs

WAIS	an abbreviation for Wide Area Information Service, an Internet search utility for locating documents or files
Web browser	computer software that allows a user to view graphics and hear the audio portions of Internet documents that contain them as well as moving from one document to another via hypertext links
World Wide Web (WWW)	the part of the Internet made up of the documents connected to one another through a series of hypertext links that are part of the documents
zipped	*See* compressed.

Part Two:
The Sites

Food

The new or the experienced traveler has myriad places to explore on the Internet. Food is a rapidly expanding Internet area that covers every facet of food and the food industry. Not only are food-related sites a rich source of information, they are welcoming. Their friendly and informal tone invites us in to the cyberkitchen for a cup of tea and a warm scone. In this broad sampling of flavors, customs, history, and recipes, you're sure to find your favorite gastronomic delight.

FOOD TALK AND HISTORY

This section highlights Internet sites that provide general food talk and information. It gives you a look into the history and development of food styles and historical periods as well as touching on the social and economic impact of food and food producers.

Don't Panic—Eat Organic

http://www.rain.org/~sals/my.html

Organic food is an increasingly important component in today's world of food and restaurants. For this reason, we thought this site (see Figure 2.1) would help round out your food knowledge. This comprehensive organic gardening Web page has excellent links to products, legal issues, and research in the areas of organic foods, biological pest control, and organic farming. If you are interested in the how-tos of organic gardening, check out the links to <u>Gardeners' World</u> or <u>Organic Gardening</u>. If you want to focus more on legal issues or are looking for government publications or regulations on this topic, move on to the links to the <u>National Biological Control Institute,</u> <u>California Organic Food Law,</u> or <u>C.F.S.A. Publications of Interest</u>

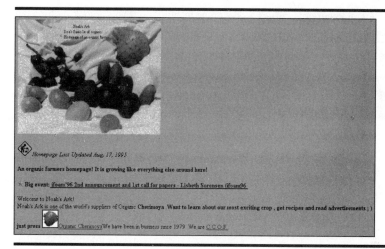

Figure 2.1:
Are you
wondering
what's in
your fruits
and vegeta-
bles, besides
fruits and
vegetables?

(the Consolidated Farm Service list of publications). The appeal of this site is its combination of down-home, earth-friendly science and its introduction to sophisticated ideas, legal issues, and techniques relating to organic fruits and vegetables.

To keep fruits and vegetables as fresh and tasty as possible you need to store them in the temperature-controlled drawer, or "crisper," in your refrigerator. Not only does this compartment control the temperature more satisfactorily for fruits and vegetables, it also slows down moisture loss so that everything stays fresher longer.

Cooking Discussion

rec.food.cooking

Do lobsters scream? Do you know any good restaurants in Denver? Any good cookbook recommendations—especially for gluten-free recipes? You'll find discussion of these burning issues and more at this site, which is a foodie's dream. Peruse the ongoing threads labeled "What did you have for dinner?" or "rude guests." Lively conversations about the propriety of tasting wine before pouring it for guests, what to do when you get the ear of corn with the worm in it, and what to cook when you get home from work exhausted (that's our kind of topic). You'll also find a lot of practical information, ideas, and opinions on topics such as kitchen design, how to select kitchen equipment, and correct food storage techniques. If you're looking for what to do with cabbage, where to order Key Limes, or how to make homemade yogurt, this is the place to come.

 Be sure to check out the FAQ at rec.food.cooking *for information on measurement conversions and recipe item substitutions. Because the Internet is a worldwide processor and disseminator of information, you may be required to make some additional calculations or changes in recipes from other parts of the world.*

Pairing Food and Wine

If you're in a quandary over which wine to serve at your next soiree, here are some general guidelines that should help you.

- Experiment. See what combinations appeal to you. You may not care for the intensity or flavors that result in certain wine and food combinations. Remember, it's your palate that you're trying to please.

- Serve any of these easy-to-drink wines—Chenin Blanc, Johannesburg Riesling, or Beaujolais—with simpler foods, such as cold cuts, fresh fruit, or lightly spiced dishes.

- Serve any of these more complex wines—Chardonnay, Pinot Noir, Cabernet Sauvignon, or Merlot—with more complex foods or foods with heavy sauces, for example, steaks, cream sauces, or wild mushrooms.

Generally speaking:

- Serve light- to full-bodied white wines such as Chenin Blanc, Pinot Grigio, or Chardonnay with fish.

- Serve light- to full-bodied white wines, such as Sauvignon Blanc or Chardonnay, or light- to medium-bodied red wines, such as Zinfandel,

Sally's Place

http://www.bpe.com/food/index.html

Sally (a.k.a. Sally Bernstein) is a chef, food writer, and generally accomplished guide to entertainment on the Internet. Her home page (see Figure 2.2) includes places to visit, restaurant reviews (organized by city), wine reviews, and a good introduction to gastronomic books, magazines, and newsletters—as well as more lengthy reviews of current award-winning cookbooks. If you're trying to locate food-related organizations such as The American Institute of Wine and Food or Meals on Wheels, you'll find them here. Sally also offers a directory to professional pastry and confectionery schools and a comprehensive (and we do mean comprehensive) look at a selected ethnic cuisine (currently from Thailand).

Pinot Noir, Chianti, or Rhone, with veal, chicken, pork, or ham or with any dishes that have a red sauce.

♦ Serve medium- to full-bodied red wines, such as Pinot Noir, Merlot, Cabernet Sauvignon, or Barolo, with lamb, duck, beef, or game meats.

♦ Serve sparkling wines before meals or with dessert.

♦ Serve Port or Sauterne after dinner or with dessert.

When you're serving wines with cheeses, follow the same general rules. For example, a medium- to full-bodied red wine, such as Pinot Noir or Cabernet Sauvignon, is best accompanied by a richer, stronger-flavored cheese such as Brie or Stilton. A light- to medium-bodied white wine, such as Sauvignon Blanc or Chardonnay, is more compatible with a lighter, less complex cheese such as Jack or Muenster. Goat cheese seems to straddle the fence, so be inventive.

The most important thing to remember when pairing food with wine is that no rules are carved in stone. For this reason, our rules are made to be broken. Find which flavor combinations suit your taste, and forget the "authorities." Your palate is often the best judge of what's "correct."

It's obvious that Sally knows her linguini from her Pinot Bianco. Her presentation is serious, knowledgeable, and great to look at. Be sure to stop.

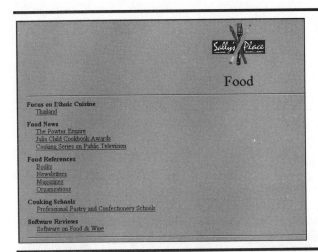

Figure 2.2:
Sally's Place is the place to be.

Carbon Steel v. Stainless Steel Knives

Two kinds of materials are traditionally used in fashioning quality knives—carbon steel and stainless steel—and each has distinct advantages and disadvantages. Carbon steel, the original metal used for knives, is softer than stainless steel. For this reason, it is easier to sharpen but tends to lose its edge more quickly than stainless. It also will rust if you don't dry it immediately after washing. Stainless steel, on the other hand, is harder than carbon steel, making it more difficult to sharpen, but it is rust free and able to keep a sharpened edge longer. When you buy knives, base your decision on the time you think you will be able to devote to keeping a sharp edge on your blades. Remember too that should you miss your mark, a finger cut with a dull knife blade results in a much nastier wound. For this reason, as well as general ease of use, we suggest you always strive for a finely sharpened blade, no matter which type is your preference.

Food Musings and History

rec.food.historic

If you're fond of cuisine from the Round Table (and we don't mean pizza), you'll want to browse this newsgroup. It is an eccentric amalgam of medieval recipes, conversations about how to make farmers' cheese, databases of pre–10th-century recipes, and questions about food from the period about AD 1200. You can search for hard-to-find ingredients (such as leavening agents from the Roman Period) and definitions of herbs and spices unfamiliar to contemporary cooks. This newsgroup is populated by friendly folks with an earnest ambition to learn about and reproduce that which has been lost or forgotten.

Improperly handled foods are a recipe for trouble. Proper handling of food and equipment is always necessary to prevent food poisoning. For this reason, always clean any cutting board between uses. It is best to keep one board for meat and another for other foods, but if this is not possible, be sure to clean your board between uses with a diluted bleach solution of one part bleach to three parts water. Acrylic cutting boards are great for meat— they're easier to clean, reducing the possibility of bacteria growth.

International Food Information Council

http://ificinfo.health.org/homepage.htm

The International Food Information Council (IFIC) is an educational foundation designed to help consumers make informed food choices. This organization offers information and ideas of interest to health professionals, educators, and parents, including scientific research, and curriculum guides and materials on a wide spectrum of food issues. The IFIC home page (see Figure 2.3) is full of straight talk on eating healthy and provides tips and suggestions for children and pregnant women. We think it is an excellent resource for all consumers, health-related professionals, and educators. Check it out.

Figure 2.3: The IFIC home page offers an array of information for all professional and nonprofessional consumers of food and food-related products.

Food and Beverage Business Directory

http://www.webcom.com/~pvo-plus/F-B/Professional.sht

Looking for that perfect basketful of dried fruits and nuts with perhaps a little cheese and crackers thrown in or for an easy way to find out more about the American Institute of Wine and Food? The Blue Directory of Food and Beverage Business is a good place to begin any food-related search. This

Know Your Olive Oils

Have you ever stood and stared blankly at a grocery store shelf full of different olive oils? It can be quite confusing trying to select the right one for your next vinaigrette. Not only do olive oils come in a variety of colors, they also range in quality and price. Olive oil is graded in two ways: first, by the process used to extract the oil, and second, by the amount of oleic acid in the oil itself. The finest olive oils are made from hand-picked olives and are cold pressed. This is the traditional method of extracting the oil from the fruit and is done with large, circular stone presses. No heat or chemicals are used. This natural process produces an oil with a lower amount of oleic acid and a higher quality, more complex, and robust flavor. In some instances, the level of oleic acid can be altered by the use of chemicals, so you should always check for the designation *cold pressed* when looking for a higher quality oil. You will find the finer oils categorized as Extra Virgin or

Peeling Garlic the Easy Way

Do you avoid using fresh garlic because it's just so darn hard to peel? Well, next time try it this way and see if the chore isn't infinitely easier.

1. Separate the garlic clove from the head.

2. Lay the clove on a cutting board and give it one or two good raps (just enough to crack the shell) with the flat bottom of a saucepan.

3. Cut off the root end and peel off the skin.

After peeling, you may smash or mince the clove with a knife. If you want to get ahead of the game, peel a whole head of garlic at one time. Then immerse the cloves in water or oil and store in a tightly closed container in the refrigerator. This way you have peeled garlic on hand to chop or mince as needed.

directory refers you to a host of associations, organizations, gift-delivery services, educational centers, research and development centers, restaurants, and more. It's an excellent place to browse whether you're a cook, a retailer, or a food wholesaler.

Virgin. The lesser quality and blander-flavored oils are generally extracted from previously pressed olives (this is called a second pressing) with the aid of heat and chemical solvents and almost always, contain a higher percentage of oleic acid. Olive oils of a lesser quality and flavor are labeled Pure or simply Olive Oil.

Olive oils are classified as follows:

◆ Extra Virgin Olive oil is cold pressed and has less than 1% acidity.

◆ Virgin Olive oil is cold pressed and has 1.01% to 1.50% acidity.

◆ Pure Olive Oil has 3.1% to 4% acidity.

Do a taste test by dipping a crust of sweet French bread into each type. You will be amazed at the difference in flavor. Choose olive oil according to your cooking needs. Keep some mild-flavored Pure or Virgin oil around for cooking and some stronger Extra Virgin oil for salad dressings or special cold dishes.

Planet Frac

http://www.lavamind.com/frac.html

Have you been to the Planet Frac? Probably not! Well, we recommend it (see Figure 2.4). Take a break from your serious search for the perfect chocolate chip cookie recipe, and enter the world of food fiction on the planet of the Veggie Piddles (intelligent vegetable creatures). You'll find this light-hearted adventure replete with whimsical graphics and a not-so-subtle moral. Be sure to follow the story to its end to find out what happens to the good-natured Veggie Piddles who eat nothing but lemon pudding and drink nothing but the wine of the vine. In fact, we recommend you pour yourself a glass of your favorite wine of the vine before you go on this adventure.

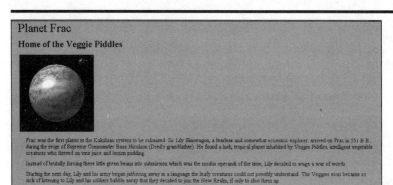

Figure 2.4: The Planet Frac offers comic relief.

Medieval Feast Anyone?

http://fermi.clas.virginia.edu/~gl8f/food.html

Do you have guests arriving shortly for their authentic medieval-style breakfast and you just can't find the right recipe? Search no more! That recipe is here at the Medieval/Renaissance Food page (see Figure 2.5).

The consensus among participants at this site is that cold porridge, sliced and fried, would be ideal. The real dilemma (which is also addressed here) is: With what should this fried porridge be served and eaten since forks and plates are not yet the convention? Such are the challenges when you attempt to accurately replicate a simple medieval repast.

This is a fascinating place to visit because of its caliber of knowledge and information. If you're trying to figure out what the proper menu items and decorations should be for your next Norman feast, we're sure you can get help here. Food is only one topic in this guide to the medieval and renaissance periods. Conversation, problem solving, and history also abound. For more information regarding food and customs from this period, we refer you to http://fermi.clas.virginia.edu:80/~gl8f/cariadoc/cooking_from_primary_sources.html.

Figure 2.5:
Recipes and Food
Service from a more
chivalrous time

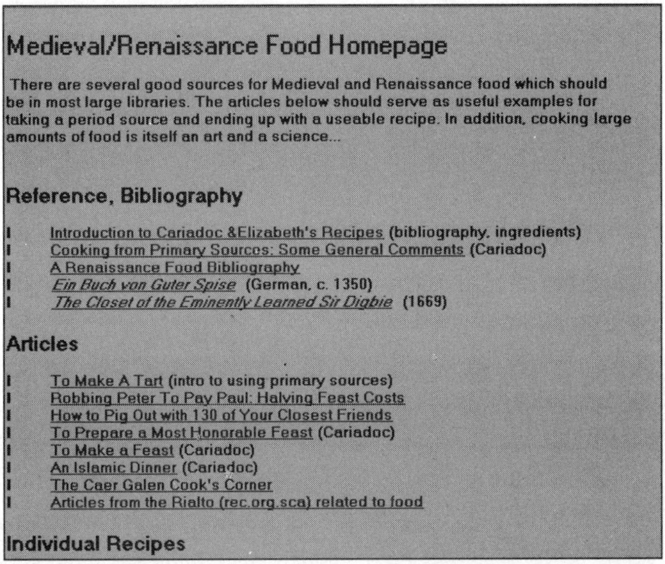

Medieval/Renaissance Food Homepage

There are several good sources for Medieval and Renaissance food which should be in most large libraries. The articles below should serve as useful examples for taking a period source and ending up with a useable recipe. In addition, cooking large amounts of food is itself an art and a science...

Reference, Bibliography

- Introduction to Cariadoc &Elizabeth's Recipes (bibliography, ingredients)
- Cooking from Primary Sources: Some General Comments (Cariadoc)
- A Renaissance Food Bibliography
- *Ein Buch von Guter Spise* (German, c. 1350)
- *The Closet of the Eminently Learned Sir Digbie* (1669)

Articles

- To Make A Tart (intro to using primary sources)
- Robbing Peter To Pay Paul: Halving Feast Costs
- How to Pig Out with 130 of Your Closest Friends
- To Prepare a Most Honorable Feast (Cariadoc)
- To Make a Feast (Cariadoc)
- An Islamic Dinner (Cariadoc)
- The Caer Galen Cook's Corner
- Articles from the Rialto (rec.org.sca) related to food

Individual Recipes

Medieval and Renaissance Periods

http://fermi.clas.virginia.edu:80/~gl8f/cariadoc/cooking_from_primary_sources.html

The participants at this Web page are true devotees of all things medieval and renaissance. You'll find some extremely interesting and scholarly conversations about ingredients, customs, and recipes of this period.

Whether you're throwing a feast for 130 intimate friends and need a menu, looking for 13th-century Islamic recipes, or researching which kind of cinnamon is most similar to that used in medieval Europe, you'll find what you seek here. If you'd like to learn more about the medieval and renaissance periods, check out the link to <u>The Society for Creative Anachronism's Arts and Sciences</u> home page at   http://www.ecst.csuchico.edu:80/~rodmur/sca/arts-sciences/.

Well-Preserved Foods

rec.food.preserving

If you want to enjoy the bounties of summer all winter long, read further. Every time we visit this site, we feel like picking a bushel of peaches to put up for the winter. Participants here are both first-time and many-time pre-servers of strawberries, tomatoes, pickles, and the like. Their discussion is useful and offered in a friendly tone. You will find tips on how to preserve fruits and vegetables safely in jars and cans as well as guides to recipes and helpful publications. We found the recommendations for beef and turkey jerky recipes particularly interesting, especially because they took the mystery out of those 25¢ sticks of meat we used to buy at the corner grocery. Be sure to peruse the FAQ for more detailed information on the process of canning and preserving.

If the Seal Fits, Use It

Not enough can be said about following proper procedures when canning fruits or vegetables. Some basic rules are:

♦ Use only firm, fresh, unbruised, fully ripened fruits and vegetables that have been washed thoroughly.

♦ Be sure all your canning equipment is clean and in perfect working order.

♦ Before you start canning, be sure that both jars and lids are immaculately clean.

♦ After processing food in jars, close lids tightly and allow them to seal. Test the seal after cooling by turning the jar upside down.

A larder full of canned fruits and vegetables is a rich bounty. You can get more detailed canning instructions from books devoted specifically to that topic. When you are stocking your pantry, be sure to follow the procedures in those books to the letter.

Did You Say Sourdough?

rec.food.sourdough

Have you heard of the ritual commonly called "sourdough worship"? The temple resides at this address. Housed inside are questions and answers to just about every facet of the development, chemistry, and flavor of sourdough and the resulting breads and rolls it helps raise. If you are just a boring old bread baker who's never used this magic leavening agent, sourdough could reveal to you a road not yet taken. It looks to us like a tasty journey. Check it out.

More Food Talk

alt.cooking-chat

You are trying once again, to avoid opening that box of macaroni and cheese for your kids' dinner, and you can't find the phone number for the local 12-step program for take-out addicts anonymous. Take a deep breath, this newsgroup may be your answer. Although less frequented than some other food newsgroups, it contains much useful information, recipes, and amicable talk. The most interesting items at the time of this review were an evaluation of various types of nonstick cookware and a bride-to-be's desperate search for a recipe for Devonshire Cream (try it dolloped on those proverbial versatile noodles). For the homemade yogurt crowd, there were some great looking recipes, not the least of which involved fresh strawberries, crushed ice, and a blender. Perfect for a breakfast treat. As usual, a resident weirdo was looking for information about how to cook a gopher snake. Oh, well.

Chefs Are Us

alt.food.professionals

Professional chefs and would-be chefs will want to explore this newsgroup. The talk here is a bit more bottom line, with questions about correct procedures for taking inventory and costing-out menu items. If you are toying with the idea of going into the food profession, this is a good place to get advice on how to get started or to find out if your fantasy matches the reality. We enjoyed getting a bird's-eye view of what happens behind the scenes in a commercial food establishment. Looks like not just another pretty plate to us.

Postmark Chefs

majordomo@halcyon.com

If you are a professional chef, an aspiring chef, or a culinary educator, this mailing list is for you. It can help you stay current in the world of food. To subscribe, send e-mail to the address above with the message SUBSCRIBE VNR-CUL *your name*.

Creative Cooking

alt.creative-cooking

Yet another general food and cooking newsgroup. You will find some excellent recipes. We especially liked the one for Salad of Roasted Peppers, Olives, and Fontina Cheese. You'll also find sage (no pun intended) advice relating to cookware and its care. Add this site to your list of places to go.

General Food Talk

alt.food

Looking for the origin of the hamburger? Many theories are kicked around here. Although you may never know the real answer, this is a good newsgroup in which to pose the question. Here you'll find a mixture of food facts, recipes, chatter, and a little politics. And you'll find a lot of activity here, including a bit of hype. Beware of cooks selling recipes.

Sushi Talk

alt.food.sushi

If sushi is your passion, alt.food.sushi is the ultimate experience. Being novices in the sushi world, we were delighted to get answers to so many of our questions at this newsgroup. The chatter here is friendly and informative and laced with a serious respect for this food and the customs that go with it.

On the Other Hand, If Fast Food Is Your Thing, Check Out These Newsgroups

Here's a bunch of newsgroups that may suit your interest or lifestyle if, like most of us, you find yourself racing around at breakneck speed more often than you would like.

alt.food.fast-food
alt.food.macdonalds
alt.food.red-lobster
alt.food.waffle-house

Sushi should be eaten slowly and with some amount of contemplation and appreciation for its ingredients, for the skill that goes into making it, and for the customs it represents. It is a welcome relief from fast food and TV dinners. The participants at this newsgroup reflect this appreciation. There is more here than just food facts.

Food and Purveyors

We hope this section will whet your appetite further. It contains conversations about specific foods, how to find them, and what to do with them.

How Old Is Too Old?

Here are some general guidelines for how long you can safely store assorted foodstuffs before they are officially over the hill.

WHERE	WHAT	HOW LONG
The Freezer	Fatty fish (salmon), cooked lobster, crab	2 months
	Stew and ground meat, variety meats, meatloaf, older chicken, fish, oysters, scallops and clams in brine, salted butter	3-4 months
	Beef, lamb, young chicken, duck, turkey, unsalted butter	6-9 months
The Pantry	Canned fish, oil, unopened cereal, baking powder and soda, bouillon, evaporated and nonfat dry milk in metal container	12 months
	Most canned goods, dried legumes, freeze-dried food, salt, sugar, whole pepper	18 months
	Dehydrated food	5 years

Mimi's Cyber Kitchen

http://www.smartlink.net:80/~hiller/food/

What a great Web page this is! We got lost and roamed around for hours. Mimi's Cyber Kitchen (see Figure 2.6) is an extremely broad-based collection of links to just about any food-related information you might be looking for. It will take you to recipe collections, general food information sites, mail-order houses, restaurant listings and reviews, government publications, and a variety of other topics. It's a wonderful place to start your search for anything remotely resembling food, and it includes a wonderful collection of photographs. Plan to spend some time when you get here.

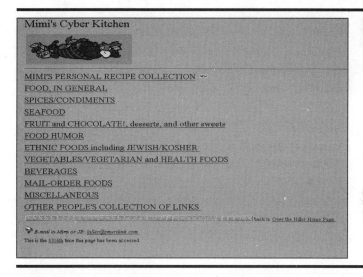

Figure 2.6:
Mimi will steer you in the right direction.

Laissez Les Bon Temps Roulez

http://www.Webcom.com/~gumbo/welcome.html

As a New Orleans–bound traveler, you may be looking for the lowdown on where to eat and what to do when you get there. This wonderfully engaging Creole and Cajun recipe page is a subset of The Gumbo Pages (see Figure 2.7), a site that strives to inform you about New

Is It Creole or Is It Cajun?

Let us clear up this great mystery once and for all. Although you'll find some of the same basic ingredients in both cuisines, Creole and Cajun are fundamentally different in style and employ different cooking methods.

First, the Creoles were the wealthier ones. Descendants of early French and Spanish settlers in Louisiana, they were by and large the rich planters and as a result developed a grand cuisine with kitchens staffed by chefs imported from Europe. Creole cooking combined locally available foodstuffs with classic French cooking techniques.

The Cajuns are descendants of about 4000 Acadians (French settlers in Canada) who were forcibly transported by the British to Louisiana in 1755. The word Cajun is derived from the term Acadian. The Acadians were a poor group of hard-working people, living under difficult conditions. Their cuisine is a result of having to rely on ingredients they had on hand. It tends to be spicy, flavorful, and cooked in one pot.

Orleans, with an insider's eye. It brings to life the special magic surrounding Creole and Cajun cuisine, as well as the overall culture and ambiance of this city. Chuck Taggart, the man behind the scenes at this address, exudes his love for Cajun and Creole cooking in every recipe and bit of information. He begins with the basics of Creole and Cajun ingredients—what they are, how to prepare them, and where to find them. From there, he leads you to recipes both simple and complicated, to articles on the history and origins of these cuisines, and to some of the inside gossip about the top New Orleans chefs and their restaurants. Among the many fascinating peeks into the New Orleans culture is a note about the creation of Blackened Redfish by Chef Paul Prudhomme and how its instant popularity led that particular species of fish to the brink of extinction. This Web site is packed full of anecdotes, humor, and advice. Spend some time here looking around.

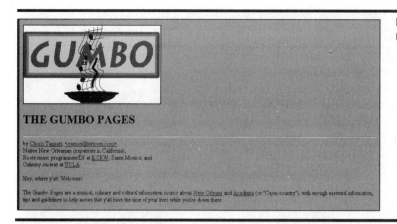

Figure 2.7:
Gumbo is life.

Herbs and Spices

http://www.teleport.com/~ronl/herbs.html#Index of Herbs and Spices

We are looking forward to the completion of this Web site. The illustrations and descriptions in the Index of Herbs and Spices are informative and visually appealing. We think you'll like browsing through the broad-based booklist. Checking back to this address from time to time is a must.

How About a Little Nosh?

http://jaka.nn.com:80/~scott/bagels

If bagels are your thing, look here for a brief history of this holey bread and tips on freezing, storing, rejuvenating, and cooking. When you delve further, you may learn correct eating protocol, nutritional value, how to order online, and how to avoid nasty cuts when slicing. Even Ann Landers has a few words to add concerning bagel safety. And you thought all there was to know about bagels was that they taste good with cream cheese! Hey, get a clue!

Red Beans and Rice

Our thanks to Chuck Taggart of The Gumbo Pages for this deliciously authentic recipe, which is traditionally served on Mondays.

1 lb. red kidney beans or small dark red beans, dry

1 large onion, chopped

1 bell pepper, chopped

5 ribs celery, chopped

As much garlic as you like, minced (CT recommends lots, 5 or 6 cloves)

1 large smoked ham hock, 1 big chunk of Creole-style pickle meat (pickled pork), 3/4 lb. smoked ham, diced, for seasoning

1 to 1 1/2 pounds mild or hot smoked sausage or andouille, sliced

1/2 to 1 tsp. dried thyme leaves, crushed

1 or 2 bay leaves

As many dashes Tabasco as you like, to taste

A few dashes Worcestershire sauce

Creole seasoning blend to taste, OR, red pepper and black pepper to taste

Salt to taste

Fresh Creole hot sausage or Chaurice links or patties, grilled or pan-fried, 1 link or 1 patty per person (optional)

Soak the beans overnight, if possible. The next day, drain and put fresh water in the pot. Bring the beans to a rolling boil. Make sure the beans are always covered by water, or they will discolor and get hard. Boil the beans for about 45-60 minutes, until the beans are tender but not falling apart.

Add everything else and, if necessary, enough water to cover. Bring to a boil, then reduce heat to a low simmer. Cook 2-3 hours at least, until the whole thing gets nice and creamy. Adjust seasonings as you go along. Stir occasionally, making sure that it doesn't burn and/or stick to the bottom of the pot. (If the beans are old—say, older than six months to a year—they won't get creamy. Make sure the beans are reasonably fresh. If it's still not getting creamy, take 1 or 2 cups of beans out and mash them, then return them to the pot and stir.)

Serve generous ladles-ful over hot, white long-grain rice with good French bread and good beer. I also love to serve grilled or broiled fresh Creole hot sausage or Chaurice on the side. Do not serve with canned beet salad, like my mom always used to do.

I like serving a few small pickled onions with my red beans—I chop them up and mix them in with the beans. It's great.

Breakfast Cereal Discussion

alt.cereal

If you're a parent, you probably think you know more than you ever wanted to about cereal (yes, the kind you find on the grocery shelf). But once you visit this newsgroup, don't be surprised if you are drawn in to this topic against your will. Here you will find reviews of the cereal items lining your supermarket shelves, information on where to get little-known cereals, and a list of the states in which only certain cereals are distributed. We found the history of the development of many breakfast cereals fascinating, particularly the part pertaining to the battle between Kellogg and Post for the title of cereal king. We've always wondered who came up with the brilliant idea to add marshmallows and chocolate to our breakfast menu, and after visiting this site, we have the inside scoop—cereal trivia abounds. If you collect cereal boxes and toys, you can discuss your hobby here. It is refreshing to find that humor abounds when it comes to this dry topic.

Ay Caramba, Pass Me the Burrito!

http://www.infobahn.com/pages/rito.html

Burrito is Mexican for: Complete proteins (beans and rice combined) can be inexpensive, quick, and delicious. Take your flour tortilla, fill it with a spoonful of beans, a spoonful of rice, and your choice of meat and garnish with salsa, cilantro, sour cream, and a bit of guacamole, and you are *really* cooking. For those of you who have never had the pleasure of biting into a steaming hot burrito, this Web page (see Figure 2.8) may be the beginning of a new adventure. The burrito is presented here with some excellent serving suggestions and a lot of humor. After perusing the recipes at this site, check out the mock menu from which to build your own online personal preference burrito. As a result of your ingredient choices, you will be privy to a personality profile and analysis (after all, your choice of salsa rather than guacamole must say something about your state of mind). After being psychoanalyzed, you should check out some of the links. Although not numerous, they will take you around and about the origins and history of the burrito and are sure to make you laugh.

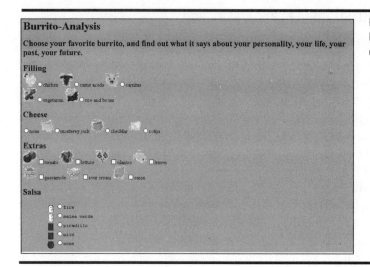

Figure 2.8:
It's what's inside that
counts.

The Wonderful World of Cheese

http://www.efn.org:80/~kpw/cheesenet95/

We were excited to find such a fitting tribute to this worldwide food. Cheese has been made in almost every culture for thousands of years, be it from the milk of cows, reindeer, goats, sheep, or camels. CheeseNet95 does it justice (see Figure 2.9). You will be taken on a complete tour of the world of cheese, starting with a general history and description of the types and how each is made. Should you choose to delve further, and we suggest you do, you will find more detailed descriptions of specific cheeses, their production methods, and flavors. A good explanation of how variables in the manufacturing process determine a cheese's particular flavor and texture is provided. If you're a health-conscious reader (and most of us try to be these days), an easy-to-understand description of how cheeses are categorized according to butterfat content and which cheeses fall into those categories will help you make personal selections. There is also a brief glossary of cheese terminology, as well as some excellent photographs that we found particularly helpful and informative.

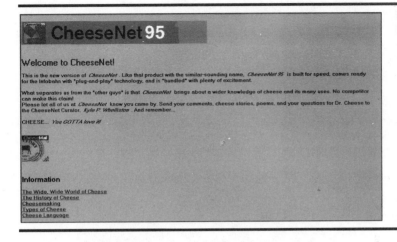

Figure 2.9:
Say cheese.

Some Like It Hot ... Some Like It Hotter

http://chile.ucdmc.ucdavis.edu:8000/www/chile.html

Chile enthusiasts of the world now have a place to unite! The Chile-Heads home page (see Figure 2.10) is definitely one of the food highlights on the Web. It's chock full of information, from descriptions of varieties and flavors to an extensive recipe archive. The restaurant and book reviews, although few in number, are thoughtfully conceived. If you're so inclined, check out instructions on how to make a Chile Pepper Ristra or find out just what botanical phenomenon makes chile peppers so hot. In a traveling mode? Peruse upcoming festivals arranged by date and locale or the restaurant guide organized by city. The tone of the Chile-Heads home page is friendly, helpful, and enthusiastic for all things hot and spicy.

Say Cheese

You often hear the terms Double Cream (or Creme) and Triple Cream (or Creme) in reference to cheese. These terms refer to the fat content in the cheese (and accordingly, how guilty you will feel when you eat it) and, generally speaking, how creamy, buttery, or rich tasting it is.

- Double Cream cheese has a butterfat content of 60% to 70%. Examples are Brie and Coulommiers.

- Triple Cream cheese has a butterfat content of 70% or more. Examples are Explorateur, St. Andre, and Saga Blue.

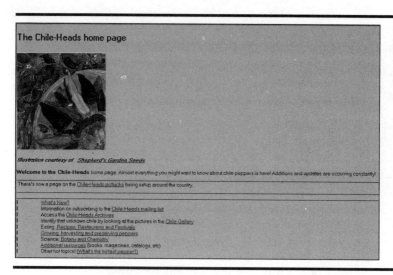

**Figure 2.10:
Chile-Heads
know what's
hot.**

The graphics are colorful and of excellent quality. Whether or not you're a Chile-Head, you'll spend a good evening or three roaming around this site.

For Hotheads

chile-heads-request@chile.ucdmc.ucdavis.edu

If you like it hot and spicy, this is the mailing list for you. It's for people interested in foods that contain chile peppers.

To subscribe, send mail to the address above with the message SUBSCRIBE.

Being Squiddish

http://www.mindspring.com/~Webrx/squid/squid.html

For the food lover, this Web page (see Figure 2.11) is a quick bite and run, that is, unless you have a more compelling interest in squid as a marine animal. The recipes, which have been pulled from rec.food.cooking, are few, but sound delicious and provide a look into the preparation of this strange-looking delicacy throughout the world. Alas, if you fail to find the perfect squid recipe here, check out the graphic at Squidley's Reef. It's way cool.

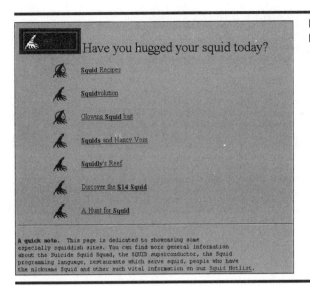

Chocolate, Chocolate, Chocolate

alt.food.chocolate

Although to many chocolate is a serious topic, the online chatter at this site is friendly with a touch of humor (proof positive that chocolate is helpful in treating depression). If you're looking for hard-to-find brands of chocolate or for help on how to correctly employ chocolate in your next recipe, you will find the people here very helpful. The conversation in this newsgroup is driven by love of one thing—chocolate. So if you share this passion, this is your place.

What Is White Chocolate?

White chocolate is not really chocolate at all. It is a blend of cocoa butter, milk solids, sugar, and flavorings. What makes it different from regular chocolate is that it has no chocolate liquor. Some white chocolates are made with a blend of oil and cocoa butter. We recommend you steer clear of those because they are not as high quality as the ones with cocoa butter only.

Lady Godiva Never Had It So Good

http://www.godiva.com/recipes/chocolatier/index.html

Godiva Chocolates and *Chocolatier* magazine have teamed up to bring you the Godiva home page (see Figure 2.12). Although Godiva previews the many wonderful products it sells (with forms for online ordering), we found ourselves drawn to the recipe archives, articles, and cooking tips provided by such a first-class periodical as *Chocolatier*. So inviting were the "Scoop du jour" ice cream sundae recipes that it became necessary for us to rush out and buy a pint of chocolate ice cream and a bunch of bananas (now we know why some grocery stores are open all night). The descriptions of types of chocolate and in which situations they are best used were interesting and informative. Tips on proper melting and tempering techniques were easy to follow. Recipes are rated according to preparation difficulty, which we also found helpful. This site is a slick production, offering lots of good advice and ideas.

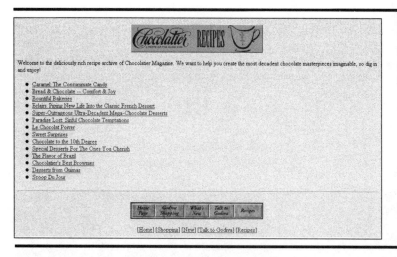

Figure 2.12: All the latest breaking news on chocolate

Serious About Chocolate?

http://www.iia.org/chocolate

Another example of the universal appeal of chocolate is presented in the Chocolate Lover's page. It is primarily a guide to commercial chocolate-related sites on the Internet. Each site name is followed by a brief description of the site's product line (eveything from truffles to cheesecake). In addition to the commercial sites, you will find a smattering of noncommercial home pages created merely for the love of chocolate. Here you will find lots of general information, including tips on cooking with chocolate, sources for equipment, and chocolate history and information.

More Chocolate, Chocolate, Chocolate

rec.food.chocolate

Do not visit this site if you are dieting. We found ourselves running to the kitchen cupboard to see if we had any more chocolate chips to munch on. This newsgroup features the fifth basic food group, chocolate. Its members are full of information about this well-loved and much-respected topic. You will feast your eyes (and stomachs) on some wonderful recipes and find a great amount of wisdom and research on the topic. We were especially intrigued by the many variations on that old favorite, Chocolate Mousse, and the ongoing conversation about M&M's. (Did you know they now come in a variety of new colors? Most notably blue—which seems altogether an unappetizing food color to us.) The chat here is friendly and seriously driven by the love (and addiction to) chocolate.

Ciao, Bella, Have a Meatball

http://www.eat.com

If Ragu's sauces are as good as its home page, we're all in luck. Mama's Cucina (see Figure 2.13) is the Web page for Ragu products, and her kitchen is always open. She provides an excellent cooking and pasta glossary, including good descriptive photographs, and a peek at her private recipe file that covers everything from appetizers to desserts. Mama is also a travel guide, sharing her personal recommendations for restaurants and hotels throughout Italy. A feature of this site that we think you will really appreciate is the collection (contributed by participants in this site) of recommended places to dine and stay in various Italian cities. Recommendations were up to date and full of tips and anecdotes. Last but not least, Mama is generous. Enter her contest and win a free trip for two to Italy.

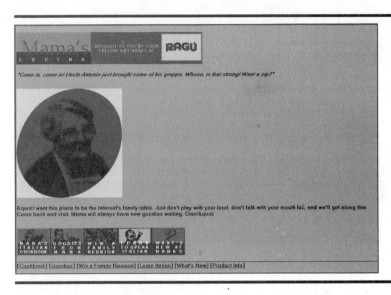

Figure 2.13:
Just ask
Mama.

The Stinking Rose

http://broadcast.com:80/garlic/garlic.htm

What would life be without the pleasures of the stinking rose? The Garlic Page (see Figure 2.14) is dedicated solely to garlic and its uses. It is a compendium of recipes, garlic-related articles (many pertaining to the medicinal properties of garlic), growing tips, and announcements. Find out about the garlic train, which is the best way to get to the Gilroy Garlic Festival, and what to do when you get there (eat garlic, of course). Check out the FAQ for a complete overview of garlic propagation and cultivation. After you're finished browsing, go roast up a few cloves and spread them on some French bread. Delicious.

Beautifully Delicious

http://www.pathfinder.com/@@Ooz654AWhgAAQBYe/twep/kitchen/

The Virtual Kitchen (see Figure 2.15) is in four beautifully put together sections: In Season, Ask the Chefs, Cooking Class, and Real Food. (Wear your hard hat at this one; it's still under construction.) This site is being developed by Time-Warner Publications, and it has left no stone (or page)

Figure 2.14:
"What garlic
is to salad,
insanity is to
art."
Augustus
Saint-
Gaudens

unturned in providing you with resources to its cooking library, recipe archives, and recently published cookbook reviews. The month we visited, the cooking class (with featured guest chef) offered coaching on the fine art of the barbeque, with an appetizing sampling of recipes, instructions, and tips on how to get the best use out of your grill and which kinds of fuel are optimal. The archives, arranged by month and topic, contain previous cooking classes in case you missed something of interest. The Virtual Kitchen is slick, clean, and professional. Take notes while you peruse it—there's lots of good information to be had.

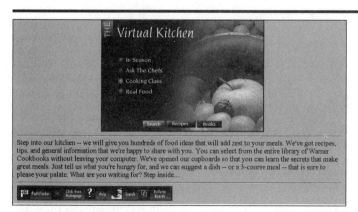

Figure 2.15:
Time Warner
Publications has
perfected the vision
thing.

Japanese Cooking

http://www.rain.org/~hutch/articles.html

If you're a fan of do-it-yourself sushi or sashimi, you'll find this Web page extremely useful. Although the photos are a little hard to decipher, the instructions are clear and easy to follow. You'll learn the difference between sushi and sashimi and how to avoid the dread parasites in raw fish that your mother warned you about. Recipes include all the basics from the correct way to prepare rice for sushi to how to make a sushi omelet (tamago), one of our personal favorites. The ins and outs of sushi rolls are clearly defined, including instructions and equipment needed, correct placement of ingredients (including diagrams) for proper rolling, and a host of possible ingredient combinations. How-to facts are presented in an easy-flowing format that makes these delectable treats accessible to even the most inexpert hands. Browse this Web site further to get a brief cultural overview of the Japanese customs surrounding these foods as well as information about where to find the best ingredients and equipment.

Osaka Sushi

http://hisurf.aloha.com/PBA/sushi/SushiHomeE.html

The Osaka Sushi Home Page (see Figure 2.16) is a pleasure for the eyes to behold. It is sponsored by the Hinode Foods Company, which has gone to great lengths to provide fascinating information and beautiful graphics. It is organized in three parts: Sushi of Seasons, The Sushi of "Festival," and The History of "Sushi." Sushi of Seasons lists the fish to be used at different times of the year, because of their freshness and abundance. Woven in are facts about fish habitat as well as a bit of fishy folklore. The Sushi of "Festival" describes the "boy's festival" and the "girl's festival," what each represents, and the type of sushi particular to each. The History of "Sushi" describes how the custom of making sushi began as way to preserve fish and the subsequent emergence of two regional styles: Kansai, originating in Osaka, and Edo, originating in Tokyo. This Web page brings you a fascinating peek into how this culinary form is so much more than its parts. It embodies the richness and resourcefulness of the island culture from which it comes.

It's All in a Name

Here's a bit of sushi vocabulary that might come in handy the next time you go to a Japanese restaurant. Knowing the names and definitions of various sushi dishes is much preferable to pointing to the one that looks good and then wondering what you just ate. After your second order of sake, however, you may not really care.

Dish	What It Is
Sashimi	Raw fish
Shoyu	Japanese soy sauce
Wasabi	Japanese horse radish
Chirashi	Assorted raw fish and vegetables over rice
Nigiri	Pieces of raw fish over vinegared rice balls
Nori-tama	Sweetened egg wrapped in dried seaweed
Tamago	Sweet egg custard wrapped in dried seaweed

Sake	Salmon
Ebi	Boiled shrimp
Hamachi	Young yellowtail
Ika	Squid
Maguro	Tuna
Tako	Octopus
Toro	Choice tuna belly
Uni	Sea urchin roe
Tobiko	Flying fish roll
Unagi	Eel
Maki-zushi	Sushi rolls
Tekka-maki	Tuna-filled maki-zushi
Kappa-maki	Cucumber-filled maki-zushi
Otoro-maki	Fatty-tuna roll
Futo-maki	A fat roll filled with rice, sweetened cooked egg, pickled gourd, and bits of vegetables
Temaki	Hand-rolled cones made from dried seaweed
Maguro-temaki	Tuna temaki

Figure 2.16:
Form and
function
abound here.

Japanese Food and Culture

listserv%jpnknu01.bitnet@listserv.net

This mailing list is for people with an interest in Japanese food and culture. It was developed and is maintained by Kinki University in Japan and has 200–300 members. Archives are available. To subscribe, send mail to the address above with the message SUBSCRIBE J-FOOD-L.

Recipes and Cookbooks

This is the place to find online cookbooks, recipe collections, and periodicals of all shapes, colors, ethnicities, and sizes. Although we're sure we've missed a few, we hope this list gives you a good overview of what's available on the Net. Keep in mind that these collections are updated daily, weekly, or monthly, so there is always something new. The good news is, you may never have to buy another cookbook.

The Foodplex

http://www.gigaplex.com/wow/food/index.htm

Merrill Shindler's Web page is a part of the E-zine Gigaplex, an online recreation and entertainment magazine. His page falls into the "Don't worry, be happy" category. It brings you pertinent data concerning the ratio of A's to Z's in a can of alphabet soup and the number of elephants in a box of animal crackers. On a slightly (and we do mean slightly) more serious note, you will find reviews of the 10 best Italian restaurants in the U.S., the 10 best Moroccan restaurants in the U.S., the 10 best hot dogs in the U.S., etc., etc. This is where Mr. Schindler's food-reviewing expertise comes in. His skill is really put to the test, however, when he takes on "weird theme" restaurants across the land, most notably, the Adam and Eve restaurant in Naked City, a resort in Indiana. If you guessed that the dress code is birthday suits, you are a very good guesser. This site is funny, quirky, and a bit offbeat. We give it three stars.

The Foodies' Online Magazine of Choice

http://www.deltanet.com:80/food/egg/index.html

An eGG is not only something to eat, it is also the acronym for the electronic Gourmet Guide. You will find this online magazine chock-full of useful information (see Figure 2.17) on topics ranging from wine and homebrewing to new kitchen gadgets (some of which you just *can't* live without). It has excellent food-preparation information in interviews with professional and amateur chefs. The Pork Belly News section concerns the economics and politics of food and delves into food pricing, restaurant sales and acquisitions, and what the weather will do to this year's vegetable crop. Not to be overlooked are the guide's cookbook reviews and coverage of recent cooking festivals, contests, and awards. Flip through these electronic pages for lots of current and interesting food-related news. Be sure to venture out from the issue at hand into some of the links.

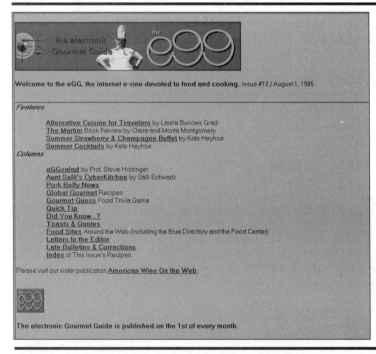

Figure 2.17:
An excellent
guide to what's
cooking

The Joy of Recipes

ftp://ftp.neosoft.com/pub/rec.food.recipes

This recipe collection is the FTP directory of recipes from the rec.food.recipes newsgroup. It is full of variety with a few eccentricities thrown in. It takes you from an Ancient Roman Menu (don't worry about finding the correct ingredients, the author offers suggested substitutions) to recipes for winter bird food. If these aren't quite what you're looking for, this site also offers a tremendous selection of recipes for the everyman (and woman), from appetizers to casseroles to chocolate brownies. We found this site offers a comprehensive catalog of menu items; its only shortcoming is being devoid of graphics, rendering it a little less visually appealing than some other sites.

Recipe Archives... An Easy Read

http://www.vuw.ac.nz/who/Amy.Gale/recipes

The recipes here cover just about any type of cuisine, including sections on special diets and vegetarian cooking. We found the recipes varied in flavor, texture, and complexity. The only drawback (and it is small indeed) to the American cook is that you'll need to convert the amounts in some recipes from the metric system. If you're looking for that favorite holiday cookie that Aunt Mabel used to make or the secret to making zucchini bread at a high altitude, you will find it in this thoughtfully organized and easy-to-browse collection. It's a great place to start any recipe search. One warning, however: Don't do it when you're hungry—unless you're willing to consume the 15-course, 4000-calorie dinner that may follow.

Just the Cooking Facts, Ma'am

news.rec.food.recipes

The topic of this newsgroup is strictly recipes. No chit-chat or long-winded explanations, just recipes. The selection is varied and comprehensive. At regular intervals, the moderators post questions from subscribers concerning how to locate certain food items. If you are looking for more conversation regarding food or a specific recipe, check out rec.food.cooking.

Indian Cooking at Its Finest

http://www.bbcnc.org.uk/bbctv/madhur/

Madhur Jaffrey brings you a tease and a sampling of her extraordinary Indian cuisine at this BBC-sponsored Web site (see Figure 2.18). Since no one is better equipped to speak about the diverse menus of regional Indian cuisine, we highly recommend you spend some time here. Ms. Jaffrey offers a small collection of recipes (you have to order the book to get more) from Punjab to West Bengal and places in between and briefly describes the area where the recipe originated and its primary culinary emphasis. You will find the tips helpful in describing or locating the proper ingredients in her recipes. There is also guidance on proper substitutions for hard-to-obtain ingredients. Little known facts about the cuisine, such as "cardamom is the vanilla of India" or "only white poppy seeds are used in India" make this collection come alive.

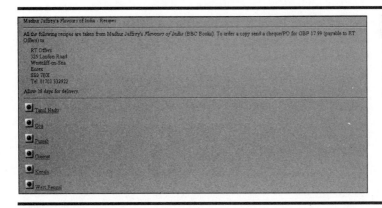

Figure 2.18: A comprehensive guide to Indian cuisine

International Recipe Collection

http://solar.rtd.utk.edu/friends/life/cookbooks/cook-record-new.html

Friends and Partners attempts to bridge the gulf between countries and cultures through the exchange of recipes. It is predominantly a collection of recipes from the countries of the former Soviet Union and the United States, but includes a limited number of recipes from other countries as well. The recipes are organized by type, for example, desserts, breads, meats, and so on. Although the collection was not large, we liked the notion of each recipe being from some person sitting in front of a computer screen anywhere from Hungary to Tbilisi to Malaysia. This Web site is not the result of one person's travels or food interest; it is truly an international effort. Although it is a work in progress, it is a great example of what the Internet is all about.

Jayne's Cyber Cookbook

http://turnpike.net/metro/sapphyr/cookbook.html

Although this site is still under construction, it has all the ingredients of one worth coming back to for new information. The graphical interface is clean, colorful, and easy to follow. Topics to be covered when the site is completed include a recipe conversion chart, cooking hints and tips, a glossary of culinary terms, and a guide to cooking basics. You will find the current recipes tasty and easy to follow, with simple preparation information and instruction provided by easy-to-read graphics. Put this site on your checklist and watch its development.

Callahan's Cookbook

ftp://suphys.physics.su.oz.au/mar/callahans/cookbook.asc

Callahan's is actually more like a moderated newsgroup than anything else. The online chatter is extremely friendly, and most recipes include a bit of personal history. Although the recipes are not in any specific organized format, they are easily browsed and vary in type and content. Some excellent cooking tips and a "quick guide to strange names" (an index of like ingredients bearing different names throughout the world) are worth reading before you begin to cook.

Dessert Recipes

http://www.aus.zanadu.com:80/GlassWings/food/recipe.html

The Glass Wings dessert page is part of a larger site found at http://www.aus.zanadu.com/GlassWings and is dedicated to the pursuit of fanciful interests. In the food pages at this site (see Figure 2.19), recipes are dished up

Shortcuts and Tips to Simplify Your Cooking Tasks

Here are some homemade tips and tricks from Callahan's Cookbook to make your food preparation quicker, easier, and less expensive.

- The Easy Way to Measure Butter. To measure 1/4 cup of butter, start with a glass measuring cup. Fill the cup with cold water until it reaches the 1/2 cup mark. Now add chilled butter until the water level reaches the 3/4 cup mark. The measurement of the butter will be accurate, and the butter won't stick to the sides of the measuring cup.

- Homemade Self-Rising Flour. This recipe equals 1 cup:
    1 cup plain flour
    1 1/2 tsp baking powder
    1/2 tsp salt

- Homemade Bisquick (self-rising flour with oil or shortening added):
    2 cups shortening or oil
    9 cups sifted flour
    1 tbsp. salt
    4 tbsp. baking powder

For both self-rising flour and Bisquick, mix dry ingredients together. Cut in shortening or oil until mixture is the consistency of corn meal. Store in an airtight container until time for use.

Figure 2.19:
The finer things
in life

Mostly Desserts and Other Culinary Atrocities

Never judge a cookbook by its cover, judge it by its dessert recipes! I believe the most important part of the five basic food groups is the dessert group. As such this area is dedicated to some of the finer things in life. Please feel free to contribute your own recipes to be included here by e-mailing me at muse@glasswings.com.au

The Chocolate Biscuits of Doom

Chocolate Chip Cookies

Fake Reese's Peanut Butter Cups

Grandma's Easy Biscuits

Holey-Moley Tabby's Guacamole

Hop on Poppy Noodles

Hotcha-cha Nachos

with simplicity in a display limited to ten at a time. We particularly liked the recipe for Chocolate Biscuits of Doom, which was accompanied by this note: "These are rich and chocolatey to the extreme. You have been warned." That being said, we think you should try this and other recipes here anyway.

Recipes from This Galaxy

ttp://galaxy.einet/galaxy/Leisure-and-Recreation/Food.html

Galaxy is an online provider of worldwide information and services. In its Leisure and Recreation section are two food-related Web pages. The first is devoted to recipes, and the second, to food in general. Both sites are actually vast lists of links to other Web sites that relate to recipes and food. There are also referrals to food-related periodicals and commercial organizations and a section devoted to new items that have appeared on the Net in the last seven days.

Cooks, Fire Up Your Ovens

http://physics.purdue.edu/~sho/recipes

You can approach this Web site from two angles, either of which will give you satisfactory results. The first approach requires you to have something in particular that you would like to cook; hence, you are going on a recipe hunt. The second assumes that you are having 10 people over for dinner in an hour and don't have any great ideas about what to cook and hope you will find something quick (*very quick*), easy (*very easy*), and inspiring here. This site is a collection of clear and simple recipes. Most have a refreshing blend of flavors and textures and won't load you down with too many ingredients to collect and prepare. You'll find the pasta salads particularly appetizing and inventive, including influences from many culinary traditions.

What's for Dinner, Mom?

http://www.public.iastate.edu/%7Eentomology/InsectsAs-Food.html

Are you tired of the same old dinner fare? Pasta, pizza, chicken, and the like? Well then, this site is what you're looking for. Straight from the University of

Iowa's Department of Entomology comes a collection of Tasty Insect Recipes (hey, this is serious). It's not an extensive collection (thank goodness), and we can't even say it's a good one. In fact, you can be sure the recipes won't be on the list in our test kitchens; however, we are committed to giving all sites equal print time, so, if you get the urge, why not whip up some Banana Worm Bread or a quick batch of Chocolate Chirpie Chip Cookies for when the kids come home from school? After all, if there was a time when catsup was considered a vegetable, why couldn't insects be considered a protein? Think about it.

Manuela's Recipes

http://he1.uns.tju.edu/recipes/

We want to have dinner at Manuela's house. This collection of small but excellent recipes will inspire even the most timid cook. Although they are not considered low fat, it won't matter once you sink your teeth into a meal planned around this Web page. You will want to start with the Bruschetta, followed by a Risotto with cheese. After a brief rest, dig into the Chicken Cacciatore with gusto, and finish it off with a dainty but delicious serving of Tiramisu. Heaven will have arrived on earth. The other alternative to dining from this site is to move to Italy. You will probably find Manuela's way a bit more economical.

Thai Cuisine

http://www.gezi.com/gzworld/recipe.html

Prapapun's Kitchen provides you with a small but eclectic collection of authentic Thai recipes. Among our favorites are Ginger Chicken, Thai Easter Eggs, and Sweet Sticky Rice with Mango. An excellent feature of this Web site is the section available for recipes from readers. The current selection on this page is Roast Duck Curry with Fresh Lychee. Not only do you get an excellent recipe, but you get some biographical notes about the authors (which in our opinion always adds to any recipe). This page (see Figure 2.20) has a friendly, humble tone that is always refreshing in the all-too-common egomaniacal world of super-star chefs.

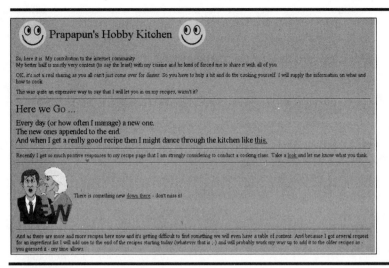

Figure 2.20:
The right
stuff

The Dinner Co-op Thing

http://www.yatcom.com/neworl/food/cooktop.html

This is what happens when a bunch of graduate students get together and try to figure out how to eat well regularly, without having to cook every day. It appears to have been a great success for them (if you're interested in how to set up a co-op of your own, they will tell you). Some members prepare dinners while other members take on the tasks of scheduling and sorting out the finances. These people really know how to cook; the recipe section here is eclectic and well versed. Some recipes are unusual, for example, the recipe for beet sauce or Moroccan chicken pie. Also included is the most delicate of all art forms—blending herbs and spices. You'll find a variety of recipes for spice mixes, including Tandoori Masala and Chinese 5 spice. If these recipes are not enough, check out the extensive links to other recipes on the Internet. This is a site you'll want to carve out a substantial amount of time to browse. Figure 2.21 shows the home page.

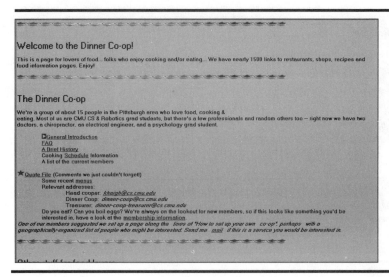

Cooking New Orleans Style

http://tatcom.com/neworl/food/recipes/breakfast

New Orleans may be well known for its jazz and the occasional political scandal, but it is world renown for its cuisine. The recipe site at this address (see Figure 2.22) is part of a more complete guide appropriately named Virtually New Orleans, which can be found at http://www.yatcom.com:80/neworl/ and contains an abundance of information regarding the city of New Orleans (including the hurricane report). The recipe collection here stocks the basics for those of you wanting to get started with New Orleans–style cuisine. Every Net site or cookbook relating to the cooking of this famous city must start with the basic recipe for a *roux*. This site is no exception; however, it is only the beginning. You will find some wonderful Red Beans and Rice recipes, as well as a classic Gumbo recipe (or three). The one we found most irresistible was Seafood Okra Gumbo, packed with copious amounts of mouth-watering seafood. Jambalaya must not be left out, of course, along with a number of other specialties we were unfamiliar with such as Calas, a fried ball of rice and dough rolled in powdered sugar (but couldn't wait to try). This site is a very good place to start your journey into the realm of this famous cooking style.

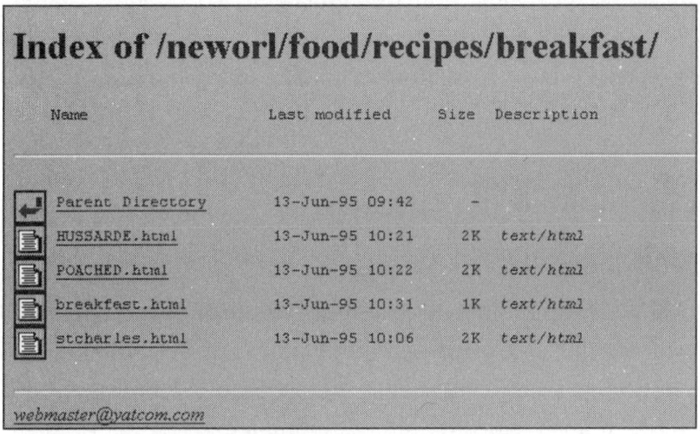

Index of /neworl/food/recipes/breakfast/

Name	Last modified	Size	Description
Parent Directory	13-Jun-95 09:42	-	
HUSSARDE.html	13-Jun-95 10:21	2K	text/html
POACHED.html	13-Jun-95 10:22	2K	text/html
breakfast.html	13-Jun-95 10:31	1K	text/html
stcharles.html	13-Jun-95 10:06	2K	text/html

webmaster@yatcom.com

Figure 2.22:
If you're traveling their way, do your pre-trip research here.

Cusines From Around the World

gopher://spinaltap.micro.umn.edu/11/fun

What you have here is an eclectic list of types and styles of food from Asia to Italy. This Gopher site is a compilation of recipes from the University of Minnesota. It includes almost every type and style of food. There's no talk or pictures, just the straight facts, figures, and ingredients. It's a good place to come when you're fresh out of creative ideas. We highly recommend the Hot Olive Cheese Puffs or the Tofu Balls as a warm-up.

The Existential Despair of Food

http://icemcfd.com/wayne/sartre-cookbook

The Jean-Paul Sartre Cookbook is a wonderful parody of both cookbooks and the existential dilemma as expounded by Sartre. The supposed intent of this "recently discovered" tome is "a cookbook that will put to rest all notions of flavor forever." In it, the author's Sartre reveals his discussions with Camus and Malraux, his problems creating an "omelet that expresses the meaninglessness of existence,"and his final search for "a single recipe which will, by itself, embody the plight of man in a world ruled by an unfeeling God, as well a providing the eater with at least one ingredient from each of the four basic food groups." Sartre's reflections in this delightful piece will have you rolling with laughter—from his attempt to enter the Betty Crocker Bake-Off to his remorse about "gaining twenty-five pounds a week for the last two months." We are eager for the next installment, which explores our life-weary traveler's love affair with the receptionist at Weight Watchers. Do yourself a favor and read this lively addition to the Net.

Cooking Slovenia Style

http://www.ijs.si/slo-recipes.html

Slovenia, a nation of two million people, sits on the sunny side of the Alps, a stone's throw from Italy. Although the country achieved independence and adopted a constitution in 1991, its cuisine has been around for generations. You will find traditional recipes as well as an introduction to the wines and beers of Slovenia at this site. The roasted "young goat with wine" turned out to be prepared similarly to our version of leg of lamb, and some pastries also had a familiar ring, among them Potica, a yeasted dough with a variety of possible fillings, ranging from chocolate to raisins to poppy seeds. This site incorporates the history, political struggles, and personality of the residents of this tiny country in a way that will make you want to go there. It seems to be a place of green hills, beautifully forested land, friendly people, and a great cuisine.

The English Server

http://english-www.hss.cmu.edu/recipes.html

The English Server's recipe folder is actually part of a larger collection of sites managed by the graduate students, faculty, and staff of the English department at Carnegie Mellon University. The author's preference at this Web page is clearly for vegetarian sites, although carnivorous sites are listed under the general category of Dead Animals. This section is further classified according to Dead Chickens, Dead Cows, Dead Pigs, Miscellaneous Dead Animals—you probably get the idea by now. Despite the obvious bias here, you will find lots of good recipes as well as links to interesting low-fat cooking mailing lists. The "greener" folks reading this book will want to take a look at this site's guide to vegetarian-friendly organizations around the world.

Vicki's Virtual Vittles

http://www.gulf.net/~vbraun/food.html

Vicki Braun is a photographer, writer, and teacher by trade, and you will become increasingly grateful that she also has an abiding interest in food when you look around her home page…it is truly a wonder (see Figure 2.23). Her recipe collection is outstanding, is very personal, and is full of easy-to-follow instructions. Most recipes are accompanied by a note about where she got them and what personal associations they have for her. In one such note, Vicki describes a lengthy search for dumplings as delicious as her grandmother's (which turn out to really be her mother's) and quips about the herb blend, ominously named "gunk," that her mother and sister concocted. The extensive recipe list is organized by category, for example, holidays, preserves, soups, salads, ethnic, and so on, and exudes Vicki's lighthearted love of food. Not only does she bring you her own recipe collection, but she has converted the Usenet Cookbook (see the entry in this section) into a database format that you can download. It has hundreds of recipes from around the world. I would say that was rather nice of her! This site doesn't stop at recipes though. It provides excellent links to other food

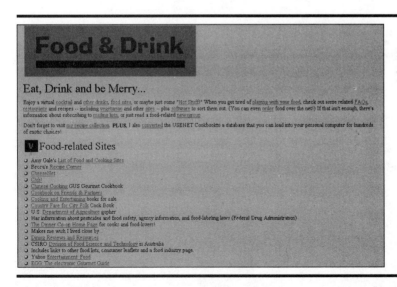

Figure 2.23: Vicki shows you the motherlode.

sites, including access to software, mailing lists, and retail pages. We award Vicki Braun the Golden Banana for her energy and creativity in bringing us this site.

Meal-Master Software

http://www.primenet.com/~wilson/mm/mealmast.html

The Meal-Master Recipe Database (see Figure 2.24) is a menu-driven software program designed to manage recipes. It can store, update, and print

Figure 2.24:
Meal-Master masters miscellaneous.

Meal-Master is a menu-driven database system especially designed to manage recipes. With Meal-Master, you can store, update, and print your recipes in a variety of formats, and you can search for recipes using any combination of Title, Category, and Ingredient criteria. *(from the manual)*

Meal-Master is a shareware program created for IBM and compatible systems by Scott Welliver and Episoft Systems. It costs $35.00 + $0.00 8.2% sales tax (WA state only) to register. It has been around for a long time (1986 if you believe the copyright date), and has a very good reputation. I have been using it for years, and have accumulated over 13,000 recipes.

Meal-Master Software Buffs

If you are using or have an abiding interest in Meal-Master software, sign up for these two mailing lists. The first is for people who use the software, and the second is for Meal-Master users to exchange recipes.

Software users can send mail to list serv@salata.com with the message SUB MM-LIST *your name*.

For recipe exchanges, send mail to listserv@alexr.demon.co.uk with the message SUB MM-RECIPES.

recipes in a variety of formats. With Meal-Master, you can search for recipes in several ways, including by title, by category, and by ingredients. Meal-Master is PC-compatible shareware, so the price is minimal. While you're at it, check out the links for Meal-Master formatted recipes on the Net. Looks to us like the choices are almost infinite.

Home Chef E-Zine

http://www.homechef.com/index.html

HomeChef Electronic Magazine (see Figure 2.25) is dedicated to providing readers with the easiest, most efficient method of preparing restaurant-quality foods at home (and they're not talking fast food). To subscribe, you complete the online form. You can pay by credit card, or you can mail in your payment. The magazine is then delivered to your e-mail address weekly. HomeChef will provide you with an excellent group of innovative recipes as well as some good basics. We especially liked the recipes for Penne Pasta with Roasted Garlic Sauce, Basil Pesto, Frozen Vanilla Yogurt with Fresh Raspberry Sauce, and homemade sun dried tomatoes. You will also find some very useful tips on cooking techniques in a section of the same name. Particularly helpful were the instructions on deglazing and reducing sauces, mincing garlic, and dicing

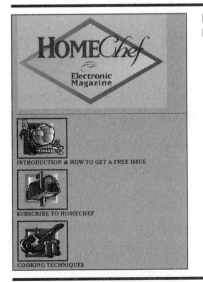

Figure 2.25:
Recent graduate from cooking school or just a reader of HomeChef?

onions and other round vegetables. HomeChef is also a guide to other useful food-related links on the Net.

The Internet Epicurean

http://rampages.onramp.net/~ricsmith/epicure.html

If you're looking for a listing of carefully chosen food-related sites on the Internet, this is a good place to begin. Loosely formatted as an online magazine, this page (see Figure 2.26) actually only steers you in the right direction as opposed to providing you with original writing and information. Links include magazine pages, commercial sites (excellent for online ordering of foodstuffs), and a plethora of restaurant sites. Checking out these links will take a while, so get up early and pour yourself a big strong cup o' joe.

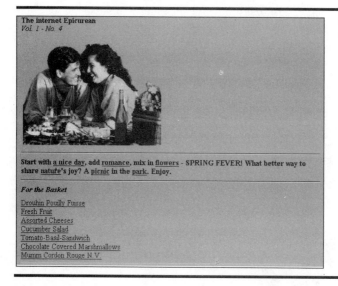

Figure 2.26:
Links, links, links

Even More Recipes, Recipes, Recipes

file://gatekeeper.dec.com/pub/recipes

This FTP site is an enormous list of recipes of all types. Alphabetically arranged, it takes you from African stew to Mexican quiche to that dessert to end all desserts, Tuscan Zucotto. If you know what you want to make but don't have a recipe, this is a great place to begin your search.

Beverages: Wine, Beer, and a Host of Others

The selection of sites dedicated to beverages is perhaps not as vast as the food selections, but nonetheless it is extensive. The enthusiasm and dedication that Netizens bring to their favorite subjects is impressive, and you will be welcomed with open arms into the newsgroups, mailing lists, and Web pages about beverages. Here is a sampling. Remember, the Internet is volatile, and sites shift all the time, so if sites appear to be missing, use the search tools available on the Web to find the new location (see *Finding Places on the Internet* in Part One.).

Why Is There Gunk at the Bottom of My Wine Bottle?

No, its not dirt that someone forgot to wash out of the bottle before filling it. There are several sources of the materials that you might find at the bottom of your wine bottle. The sludge that comes at the bottom of some bottles of aged red wine is known as sediment. It is no more than the accumulation of grape solids—skin, seeds, and pulp—that are a natural part of the fermentation process. In contemporary winemaking, most wine is filtered and fined (clarified of suspended particles with either organic—egg whites or gelatin—or chemical—bentonite or diatomaceous earth—materials) to eliminate any remaining solids from the wine that are transferred from the barrel to the wine bottle, but occasionally some sediment will remain. If you have an old bottle of red wine with sediment in the bottom, handle it gently so that the sediment is not disturbed, and consider

American Wine on the Web

http://www.2way.com:80/food/wine/

Whether you are just starting to learn about wine or you are a knowledge-able wine drinker, American Wine on the Web has something to offer. You will see discussions of a broad range of wines—from White Zinfandel to Oregon Pinot Noir. Wines produced throughout the U.S. are featured on this broad-ranging page. We never knew that wines are made in Missouri, but after reading the Midwestern USA section, our curiosity is piqued enough to go out and find some of the recommended varieties.

General Wine Discussion

alt.food.wine

Are you wondering about New Zealand wines? Do you have some questions about how long to cellar vintage champagne? Are you looking for wineries to tour when you visit the Pacific Northwest? Any question related to wines and wineries is fair game in this friendly newsgroup. There always seems to be someone with information about the subject you are interested in.

This is a great place to get recommendations from fellow oenophiles about great wineries and associated restaurants and hotels around the world. When taking off for a trip to a foreign country, it is invaluable to have a

decanting it—pouring it slowly into another container so that the sediment remains in the original bottle. Decanting the wine allows you to serve it without dispersing the sediment that has settled to the bottom of the bottle over the years, thus maintaining the clarity of the wine.

The clear crystals that are sometimes found at the bottom of a bottle of white wine are not slivers of glass, but tartaric acid crystals. Tartaric acid is a natural component of wine, and sometimes it resolidifies in crystal form in untreated wine. Besides feeling somewhat strange in your mouth, there is nothing wrong with wine that has tartaric acid crystals in it. In earlier times, before modern processes were used, sediments were a regular part of the contents of wine. Modern winemakers try to avoid them for esthetic reasons, but they are in no way indicative of "bad" wine.

specific destination in mind as a starting point. It is bad enough to endure the shock of jetlag and arrive in an unfamiliar place at what your body tells you is the middle of the night—finding your way around can be a major endeavor with signs in different languages. Having a destination where you are expected and will be welcomed can make all the difference. The shock of arriving in Rheims, France, after a 14-hour flight followed by a 10-hour drive was mitigated by a tray of French cheeses and pates and the iced bottle of French champagne that was brought to our room when we drove up at 9:45 PM.

Glossary of Wine Terms

http://metcon.met.co.nz/nwfc/beard/www/wine_glossary.html

Ever wondered what a lean, lemony Sauvignon Blanc is or an oaky, full-bodied Zinfandel? The wine world has its own special lingo that is not always clear to the uninitiated. There is an Internet source for many winemaking and wine-tasting terms—the GLOSSARY of Wine-Tasting Terminology (see Figure 2.27). In this hypertext document (see *What Is Hypertext?* in Part One*)*, the definitions are not full-blown treatises, but concise explanations, well suited to quick reference. This glossary is a handy resource for the beginner or intermediate wine drinker to use as a reference for the technical terms of wine tasting and description.

This document is also interesting for the new Internet user as an example of how hypertext works. Clicking on a highlighted word takes you immediately to the address that is embedded in the word of that term. One caveat though: The page is in New Zealand, and it takes some time to download. If you like it, you might want to save it to your disk for faster access.

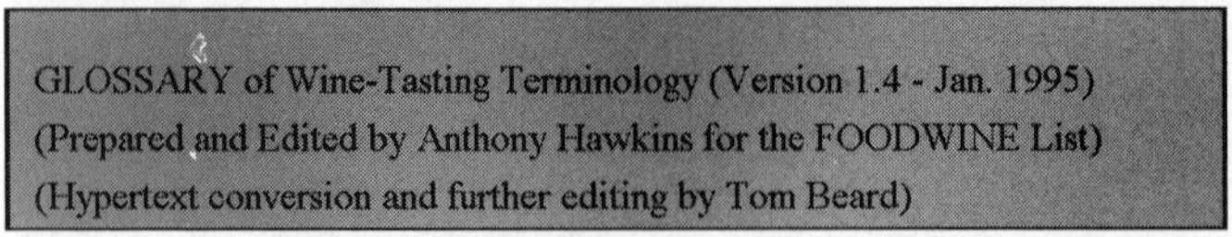

GLOSSARY of Wine-Tasting Terminology (Version 1.4 - Jan. 1995)
(Prepared and Edited by Anthony Hawkins for the FOODWINE List)
(Hypertext conversion and further editing by Tom Beard)

Figure 2.27:
The compleat wine taster's guide to wine terminology

A Place to Begin Your Bacchanalian Journey

http://augustus.csscr.washington.edu:80/personal/bigstar-mosaic/wine.txt

Are you a member of a wine-tasting group that would like to compare your tasting notes with those of others? The Wine Page (see Figure 2.28) has several collections of tasting notes that you will find useful for this purpose. The Virtual Tasting Group (see Figure 2.29) is a place to compare notes with others. You can list your own opinions of wine with others from throughout the world in a gigantic comparative tasting.

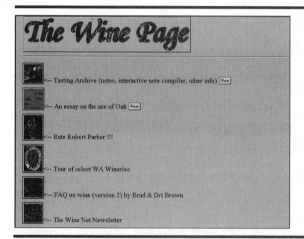

Figure 2.28:
A guide to northwestern American wines

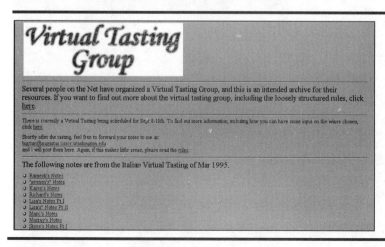

Figure 2.29:
Compare your wine tastings with those of other Internauts in the Virtual Tasting Group.

In the Tasting Archive you can record your notes and list them along with the notes of others who have tasted the same wines. The virtual approach is quite different from a real live blind tasting, but the potential for getting more input is considerable.

If you find that some notes from the other tasters use terminology unfamiliar to you, check out the FAQ on the Wine Page. The address for this extensive document (which is more easily reached by clicking on the link in the Wine Page) is http://augustus.csscr.washington.edu:80/personal/bigstar-mosaic/winefaq2.txt, and you may find the information here valuable as a resource for a wide range of winemaking and wine-tasting information.

Blind Tastings

No, this doesn't involve blindfolding people, like you did at birthday parties when it was time for Pin the Tail on the Donkey. Setting up a blind tasting is a way of having fun with your friends and teaching yourself about wines at the same time. To start, decide on a range of wines you want to taste—for instance, 1992 Oregon Pinot Noirs in the $10 to $20 price range. Appoint one of your group to go out and purchase the wines. Each fifth of wine will provide tastes for a maximum of 15 people (remember, this is a tasting), and depending on the experience of your group, you can expect to reasonably compare 6 to 10 wines. Out of sight of the tasters, uncork the wines, and cover each with a numbered bag so that each wine can be identified by number. Each taster arranges his or her glasses and numbers them with a wax pencil so that, as the wines are poured,

everyone gets the same wine in glass number one, two, and so on.

Pass out scoring sheets so that everyone can score the wines for appearance, aroma, balance, finish, and overall quality with an agreed point system. After the wines have been tasted and evaluated, add up all the scores and rank them according to the group's overall totals. Then unveil the wines in the order they have been ranked. This method guarantees a lively discussion and some real surprises. It is also helpful if you have one or two participants who have some tasting experience, not to make the final decisions, but to guide the others in the process.

If you are just starting out as a group, try tasting 5 or 6 wines rather than 8 or 10. You will be amazed how much you can get out of each wine and how the tastes of wines change over the course of an evening.

Bruce's Wine Page

http://www.pcix.com/wine/index.html

Bruce Skinner has put together an attractive wine page (see Figure 2.30), featuring an impressive collection of links to wine regions and styles around the world. In addition to the usual collection of links to domestic wine pages in California, Washington, Oregon, and New York, you will find links to pages featuring South American, South African, Spanish, Hungarian, and Mediterranean wines. There are also links to a variety of reference and wine information sources in the form of newsgroups, mailing lists, and journals that are available on the Internet. The time you spend following up the links here will be generously rewarded, since Mr. Skinner has carefully chosen his sources and does not lead us into blind alleys.

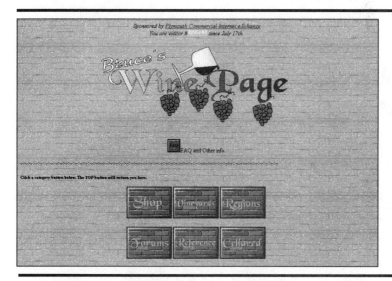

Figure 2.30:
Bruce's Wine
Page with its
numerous
resources

Ozwine: Australian Wine Mailing List

maiser@koala.cs.cowan.edu.au

Are you a lover of Australian wines? Would like to get in touch with others of your ilk? Get on the Ozwine mailing list by sending e-mail to the address above. Include a message requesting a subscription to the Ozwine. There are lots of you out there, and you don't all live down under.

The Wines of Spain

http://www.eunet.ex:80/InterStand/vino/es_vino.html

We have been enjoying Spanish wines for years: Spanish *cava* (sparkling wine) at weddings, Spanish *amontillado* sherry for aperitifs, and more recently, Spanish *rioja* (red wine) for its richness and complexity. There are many emerging wine areas in the world—Chile, Australia, New Zealand—but fine wines have been grown and produced in Spain for hundreds of years without the same notoriety and publicity of French and Italian wines. If you are at all interested in learning about the winegrowing and creating techniques of Spain, the Wines of Spain page is a good place to begin your education. The information is presented at a basic level, and there are links to sources telling you where to locate Spanish wines if you don't find them readily available.

Epicure

http://www.sf.net/epicure/epicure.html

Be sure to check out Anthony Dias Blue's informative, gracefully written commentaries on wines and wine drinking. The Epicure page (see Figure 2.31) is a link from SF Net (see the restaurant reviews in SF Net in the *Dining Out* section). A wine writer for the *San Francisco Chronicle* and numerous other publications, Mr. Blue brings a wealth of knowledge and experience

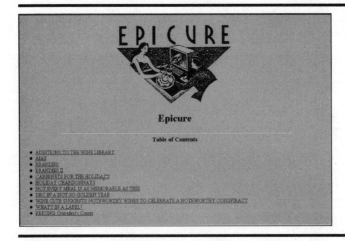

Figure 2.31:
Anthony Dias Blue's Epicure
wine essays and tips

to his essays. You will get some useful tips here for your next wine-buying expedition.

What's in a Name? American v. French Wine Names

When you go out to buy a bottle of Champagne, what will you get? If you are considering Domaine Chandon or Mumms from the California Napa Valley, your are technically buying sparkling wine, not Champagne. French wines are named for the regions in which the grapes are grown. In the United States, however, wine names reflect the type of wine. For example, in the United States, Champagne can be made from chardonnay grapes or—if its pink—pinot noir grapes, but true Champagne, according to the French, must come from grapes grown in the French region of Champagne. A bottle of Eyrie Pinot Noir is made from pinot noir grapes grown at the Eyrie vineyard in Oregon. If we wanted to buy a French pinot noir wine, we would buy a bottle of French Burgundy, grown in the Borgogne (Burgundy) region of France. Borgogne is also the region where the great French Chardonnay wines are made, so if we wanted French Chardonnay, we would look for French White Burgundy. Naming practices differ from country to country, so don't make any assumptions about what you will find. We are even seeing some changes in labeling practices. If you buy a bottle of French wine imported to the United States, it may very well be labeled Chardonnay, for the sake of foreign consumption, even though it wouldn't be considered Chardonnay in France.

A Foreign Exchange of Wine Information

http://www.ensta.fr:80/~oinos/index.html

If you like getting your wine news in French, this is the page to read (see Figure 2.32). It consists largely of requests for information and connections from people traveling to France as well as more general requests from others. The exchange is quite cosmopolitan, and the messages, while predominantly in French, contain some English. If you want to respond to someone or something you read on this page, don't hesitate to do so in English. Many of the addresses are from English-speaking countries, such as England, New Zealand, and the United States.

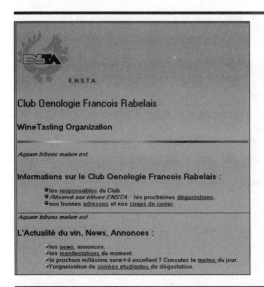

Figure 2.32:
Speaking French is encouraged here, but not required.

Wine Information from the Authorities

http://pubWeb.ucdavis.edu/Documents/WINE/ven1.html

Perhaps your interests in wine are more academic or professional than the casual interest of most tasting groups. If so, the UC Davis Web page from UC's famous Department of Viticulture and Enology—grape growing and winemaking—will interest you. This is not to say that you have to be a professional winemaker to find anything interesting here. In addition to lots of information about home winemaking and university extension classes that the department offers, a reference page lists many of the major wine locations on the Internet (wine URLs) as well as a site for downloading back issues of the quarterly journal *Viticulture & Enology Briefs*. The academic atmosphere is mixed with some fun stuff: Check out the Wine Aroma Wheel. You might want to share it with your wine-tasting group.

Making Mead

http://www.atd.ucar.edu/rdp/gfc/mead/mead.html

What is mead anyhow? It's the stuff that Beowulf and the guys consume in large quantities so that they are unconscious when Grendel appears in the mead hall to scarf them, right? In the Mead Maker's Page, you will find out that mead is a fermented alcoholic drink made with honey. It's also called honey wine. It has been consumed in large quantities over the ages by various cultures, including most northern European countries. As is the case with beers, a variety of fruit ingredients are used in making meads, including apples, grapes, spices, and—if you can believe it—chile peppers. The Mead page (see Figure 2.33) has mead recipes that use strawberries, mangos, and a range of other ingredients that you never imagined in connection with the making of mead. Of course, there is discussion of beekeeping, since bees are the producers of the primary ingredient in mead. And finally there is discussion of the various approaches to making the beverage and the pros and cons of each.

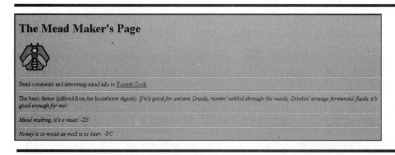

Figure 2.33:
The Thrilla
from
Vanilla—
float like
a butterfly,
sting like
a bee.

Mead Digest Mailing List

mead-digest@eklektix.com

History has it that mead making fell out of fashion about 1700. If you are of a different opinion and would like to communicate with others who share your point of view, send the message SUBSCRIBE to the address above. You will find that the community of mead makers is alive and well and interested in hearing what you have to say on the Internet.

BEER AND BREWING

The real problem with Internet pages about beer and brewing is not how to find them, but how to sort through them. The Yahoo page at http://www.yahoo.com/ Entertainment/Drinks_and_Drinking/Alcoholic_Drinks/Beer/ shows, at this viewing, links to 44 breweries, 22 companies, 7 festivals, and 24 personal Web pages. We have tried to sort through the confusion to cull out some helpful sites, but don't hesitate to look through what is out there yourself. A lot of folks are having fun creating Web pages, and the number of pages is growing like the head on a Guiness.

Command Central for Beer and Brewing Information

http://alpha.rollanet.org/

A site dedicated to the home brewer, featuring recipes, technical tips, and loads of suggestions, the Brewery (see Figure 2.34) is an excellent Web site for everyone interested in beer and brewing. It is a hub of information with connections to brewing clubs such as the Association of Brewers, The Brewery InfoBase, and home-brewing clubs throughout the United States, Europe, and Asia. This Web page, maintained by a group of dedicated volunteers, is well organized and informative and has many links to beer and brewing subjects. Online Resources provides a variety of information about

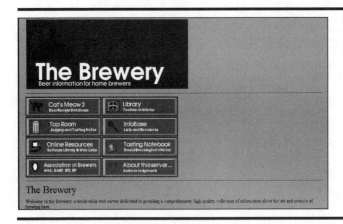

Figure 2.34:
The Brewery—a hub Web
site for beer lovers

numerous downloadable software to record and track your brewing process as well as links to other beer, whisky, and cider sites.

Additional links are to FTP and Gopher sites that have recipe archives and newsgroup addresses with the relevant FAQs about beer and brewing. You won't want to miss the frequently updated listings of U.S. festivals and competitions in the <u>Calendar of Events</u>. If you are thinking of having your own competition, be sure to look at the <u>Tap Room</u>, which contains a multitude of guidelines about how to judge and evaluate beer. Even if you are not setting up a competition, look at the Beer Style descriptions, where we can almost guarantee you will find kinds of beer that are new to you.

Another place you won't want to miss is <u>Club Net</u>, a list of Web sites maintained by brew clubs throughout the United States and Europe (see an example in Figure 2.35). Look for the number of European links to expand as more clubs see how effective this page is.

Figure 2.35:
One of the international sites to be found in Club Net—
The Metabisulphite Club in Aberdeen, Scotland

Brewing Your Own Beer

news:rec.crafts.brewing

Are you the victim of an aphid infestation of your crop of hops and wondering what you can do about it short of dusting your plants with insecticides? Perhaps you are thinking of trying to make a batch of blueberry beer, or how about some raspberry beer with a pale red luster? Maybe you are just interested in giving brewing a first try, and you are curious about what is involved. A wealth of information is available from the home brewers who frequent this newsgroup; these folks have an astonishing amount of knowledge about and experience in brewing. These home brewers are not constrained by the regulations with which professional brewers must comply, so they will try anything that strikes their fancy.

The subjects of conversation here are not limited to beer, but include ale, lager, mead, rootbeer, and cider. Technical questions concern equipment and methods. Maybe you've been curious about how to hook up the cooling mechanism of your freezer using a computer fan to keep a keg of your home brew chilled down. This is an energetic and fun newsgroup that may inspire you to try some adventures in brewing that have been on the back burner for a while.

Masters of Lighthearted Fun with Beer

http://BeerMasters.com/BeerMasters

The Beer Master's Tasting Society home page (see Figure 2.36) is provided by a group that is dedicated to enjoying beer, having fun, and not taking themselves too seriously. These folks have assembled quite a collection of services and equipment, and you can order any of it online, from their newsletter to a specially produced beer mug. Their *joie de vivre* is expressed clearly on their home page, but they are serious enough about their organization to ask for a membership fee. Various benefits accrue when you join, including a regular newsletter. They make it sound as though they are serious about having fun.

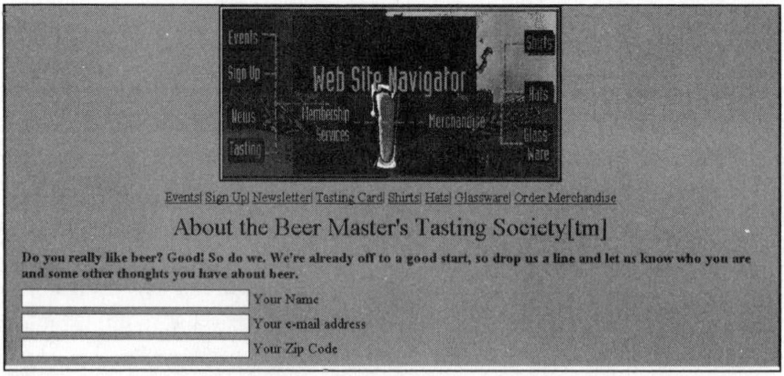

Figure 2.36 :
The Beer
Master's
Tasting
Society's
home page

Brewing Your Own beer with Professional Equipment

http://www.tcel.com:80/~gobrew/

If you are a home brewer, imagine having access to a professional brewery—the equipment, the setup, the recipes, and the knowledge. This is a possibility, and many are currently taking advantage of it. The Brew on Premise (BOP) Pages (see Figure 2.37) explore the full range of capabilities, restrictions, and rules governing such an enterprise. Home brewing is a current phenomenon in Canada, Australia, and the United States, and there is discussion here of the regulations in the places that allow it. If you are intrigued by this prospect, check out the BOP pages.

Figure 2.37: The Brew on Premise Pages is for home brewers who want access to professional breweries.

The Cat's Meow

http://guraldi.itn.med.umich.edu/Beer/cats-meow/top_page.html

Are you looking for beer or ale recipes? If so, you'll want to check out the Cat's Meow Web page, which is devoted to topics of interest to home brewers. This extensive collection of recipes has every kind of beer you can imagine. Would you like to try making some ale from blackberries, cherries, raspberries, apricots, cranberries, or apples? How about Pumpkin Bitter made with ginger and cilantro? This is the place to get directions for how to go about it. As the introductory notes specify, however, "This collection is, of course, provided as-is with absolutely no warranties of any kind whatsoever—Caveat

Brewor (we don't guarantee that the recipes will taste good or even that they won't make you violently ill)."

The information in this Web page is of intrinsic interest to the casual observer, not only for those interested in making beer, ale, or some other related beverage. Even though we have no real experience or even thought of trying to brew beer, we found ourselves looking through some of these recipes, trying to imagine what the process and the results were like.

Home Brewing Mailing List

llistserv@ualvm.ua.edu

Exchange recipes and chat with other home brewers about your experiences. You will have your questions answered here, and maybe you'll be able to help out others with your experience. To subscribe, send the message SUBSCRIBE BEER-L *your name* to the above address.

Growing Hops from the Ground Up

http://www.teleport.com/~gtinseth/

If you are seriously involved in growing your own hops, be sure to check out Glen Tinseth's Hop page (see Figure 2.38). If you want to find out how to analyze the quality of your current crop, you'll want to click on the links to

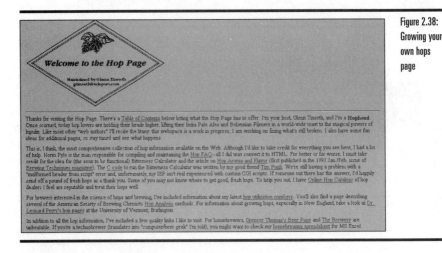

Figure 2.38:
Growing your
own hops
page

specific technical information. Additional links are to sources of more general beer and brewing information that appear to be carefully chosen for quality. An interesting tangent here is the spreadsheet for "technobrewers'" use in analyzing the brewing process and the C source code for bitterness analysis of hops. This is impressive stuff.

Beer Labels

ftp://ftp.stanford.edu/pub/clubs/homebrew/beer/images

Are you a fan of beer labels? If you are, this site will be a real find for you. Assembled here is an impressive catalog of labels of all types from all over the world. If you are a home brewer and you have bottled some of your own creations, you'll want to take a look these designs. They might spark an idea for your own label. Figure 2.39 shows one of our favorites.

Figure 2.39:
One of the images from the beer label FTP site

BEER FESTIVALS

When we think of beer festivals, the first to come to mind is the great Oktoberfest in Munich (see Figure 2.40). It's hard to imagine more fun than

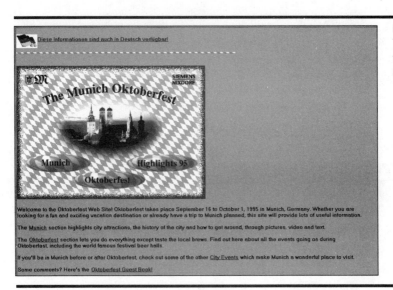

Figure 2.40 :
The grand-
father of all
beer festivals

being in the crisp fall weather in Germany, with the added pleasure of drinking world-famous German beer.

This may be the grandfather of beer festivals, but one thing that beer
drinkers around the world share is the love of having a party. You can find
out when and where those parties are on the Internet.

The Continual Beer Party

http://www.mindspring.com:80/~jlock/wwwbeer9.html

If you want to see what is happening in the world of beer festivals, the World
Wide Web Virtual Library is a good place to start. This service offers a
resource, much like Yahoo, that organizes and indexes many Net resources.
If you are looking for a listing of beer festivals to attend or if you are throw-
ing one of your own and want to send invitations, check out the World Wide
Web Virtual Library's Beer Festivals & Homebrew Competitions page (see
Figure 2.41).

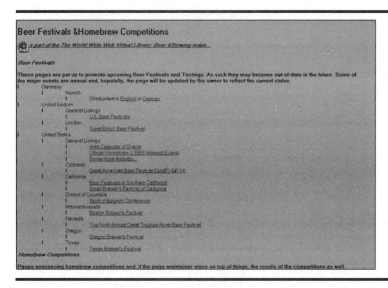

Figure 2.41 :
Where to find
the beer
festival
nearest you

Local Beer Festivals

http://www.eden.com/~erc/tbf.htm

The Texas Brewers Festival (see Figure 2.42) is one of many local events that can be found throughout the United States and the rest of the world. In the United States, we are currently enjoying a flowering of microbreweries, all of which are eager to show their wares to an equally enthusiastic public. The

Figure 2.42:
Deep in the
heart of Texas

large, national breweries are along for the ride, of course, but if you are interested in finding out about local beer activities, these festivals are a great source of information.

COFFEE AND TEA

Coffee and tea occupy special places in our culinary cultures—coffee since AD 1000 in Africa and tea since the 4th century in Asia. What is it about these drinks that makes them so significant? Certainly the caffeine content plays a major role and is used in a variety of compounds for its well-known stimulant effects. But many other food substances, for example, cocoa, also contain caffeine. Caffeine alone does not explain the central role of both drinks in the significant social events of many cultures: the elaborate Asian tea ceremonies, the British high tea, the European coffee house boom of the mid 1600s, and the omnipresent American cup of coffee. The combination of a rich aroma and the complex web of flavors exuded by tea or coffee has the power to cast something of a spell over us, which brings us back again and again for more of the same.

COFFEE

We can thank the civilizations of north Africa and the Middle East for introducing us to the custom of consuming coffee as a hot beverage. European traders encountered coffee in their expeditions to the Far East in the early renaissance, but it was not until the middle of the 17th century that coffee became available in northern Europe. Coffee houses sprang up in the metropolitan areas of England, the Netherlands, France, and Germany and became so popular that in 1675 Charles II of England issued a royal "Proclamation for the Suppression of Coffee Houses." Can you imagine the effect on modern life if the consumption of coffee were banned? Deadlines throughout the academic, corporate, and government worlds would be missed for years. Fortunately, the public outrage was such that Charles rescinded his proclamation within two weeks.

The enthusiasm for caffeine lives on and is much in evidence on the Internet in the form of numerous energetic, sometimes wild-eyed, personalized pages.

An Ode to Coffee

http://www.flightpath.com/Brento/AnOdeToCoffee.HTML

One of the more tasteful and attractive Web pages is entitled An Ode to Coffee (see Figure 2.43), designed by Brent Sleeper. (But how much can he really sleep if he works for National Public Radio, has his own business as an Internet service provider, and puts together elegant HTML pages in praise of coffee?) This page offers a sophisticated sense of humor, an excellent use of language, and a number of links to other coffee-related sites such as The Coffee Page, Mothercity Coffee (reviews of Seattle cafes), and A Brave New Coffeehouse World (a listing of Internet cafes).

Particularly amusing are the Java Jive page and Coffee, Coffee, Coffee, a glorious hymn.

An Ode to Coffee and a variety of other resources are also available on Yahoo and can be reached at http://www.yahoo.com/Entertainment/Drinks/Coffee/. As you might expect, Yahoo is a reliable central source for coffee-related information and connections to other coffee resources.

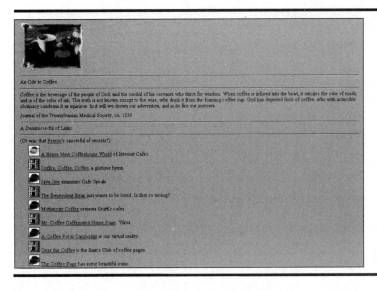

Figure 2.43:
The amusing and well-connected Ode to Coffee

General Coffee Information

rec.food.drink.coffee

Are you interested in roasting your own beans? Lots of folks do it, and some-one even posted an article about roasting beans in an air popcorn popper. The smell of roasting your own is magnificent, and if you feel that you would like some help on technique, post a message in rec.food.drink.coffee. In fact, any questions or comments regarding coffee are fair game here. You'll find discussions about growing it, making it, and consuming it; about kinds, brands, and varieties of coffee and coffee beans; about retail coffee outlets and coffee-making equipment; about how coffee is made; about how to store beans most effectively; about the effects of caffeine; and about anything else related to coffee.

A Free-Wheeling (unmoderated) Coffee Newsgroup

alt.coffee

Another newsgroup with the same focuses and topics of conversation as rec.food.drink.coffee is alt.coffee. The main difference between the two is that alt.coffee, because it is unmoderated (as are all *alt* newsgroups), entertains considerably more tangential topics. In fact, you may very well find this newsgroup invaded by Netizens who have some self-promoting or even hostile intent, completely unrelated to the subject of coffee. If you encounter this sort of ill-intentioned posting, you can ignore it or, if you are so moved, take vigilante action and respond to the inappropriateness of abusing this valuable public resource.

Worked Up About Caffeine?

http://ificinfo.health.org/faq-caff.htm

The International Food Information Council's Web page, Perspectives on the Safety of Caffeine, is a great source of information on caffeine and how it works. We know that caffeine is a drug that improves our attention, concentration, and coordination by stimulating the brain cortex. It can be a crucial element in meeting a looming deadline or staying up until the wee hours to prepare for a biology test. Some mornings that first cup of coffee hauls us out of a morass of somnolence and brings us up into the world of light, putting our functional selves back in control. That's the good news. But what about the other things that caffeine does to us, such as increasing heart rate, constricting blood vessels (thereby raising blood pressure), stimulating the secretion of stomach acids, and sending us to the bathroom to answer the demands of our stimulated kidneys and small intestine? And is that all? The International Food Information Council tells us that, in general, caffeine is benign, and that there is no cause to worry about its effects. Those of us who are caffeine sensitive may have reason to wonder about this

Making a Good Cup of Coffee

Coffee consists of two ingredients: water and coffee beans. If you want good-tasting coffee, you must store the beans properly. The oil in coffee beans is the critical flavor component that will oxidize (that is, turn rancid and bitter) if left at room temperature, making the coffee less than ideal. Store the whole beans in the freezer in an airtight container and grind them 10–25 seconds depending on your brewing method. Grind the beans just before making coffee to maximize the surface area and therefore speed the brewing process. If ground beans are exposed to the air for long periods before brewing, oxidation of the volatile oils is maximized. Ideally, you would grind beans immediately after roasting only as many as you needed, and brew the coffee right away. Since this is not practical for those of us who live in the real world, with jobs and kids and lives to get on with, we have to make some compromises. The best approach then is probably to buy a quantity of beans and store them whole.

Use the drip method or the plunger pot method to make coffee. The percolator brings out the bitterness in coffee by repeatedly passing hot water over the beans. An automatic drip maker that has a timer is a worthwhile investment—you get fresh pots of coffee at a predetermined time. If you are making drip coffee by hand, start with cold water. Hot water from the water heater contains less dissolved air and can taste flat. Heat the water to 200 degrees (just below the boiling point), pour it over the ground coffee, and drink immediately. The flavor of coffee begins to deteriorate after 20 minutes on a heat source, so if you are going to keep it, use a thermos pot. It will maintain the flavor much longer than a carafe sitting on a hot plate.

clean bill of health. The council provides nutrition information about a wide range of subjects through links to <u>Health Professionals</u>, <u>Educators</u>, and <u>Parents</u>.

Beyond Caffeine

http://www.cis.ohio-state.edu/hypertext/faq/usenet/caffeine-faq/faq.html

The chemical content of the coffee bean is remarkably complex and bears some scrutiny. If you are curious about the wealth of alkaloids that are present in coffee, and that certainly contribute to the marvelous complexity of the aroma and flavor, check out the FAQ about Coffee and Caffeine (see Figure 2.44). Available both in rec.food.drink.coffee and as a Web page, this extensive document has much to say—like the newsgroup itself—about a wide range of subjects surrounding all aspects of coffee as well as caffeine.

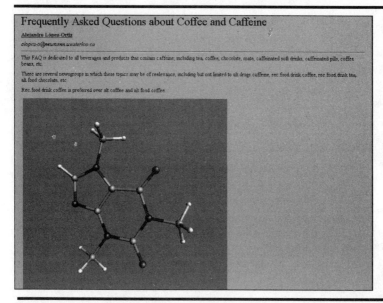

Figure 2.44: More than you ever want to know about coffee

Café Mam

http://mmink.com/mmink/dossiers/cafemam.html

Want to get away from the world of chemical pesticides? Don't miss Café Mam (see Figure 2.45), a site where you can learn about and even order organically grown, socially responsible coffee. It is produced by the ISMAM co-op, a group of native Mayan farmers living in the highlands of Chiapas, Mexico. They adhere to strict growing and production standards in order to meet the requirements for using the organic label. These folks not only supply organic coffee, they ship it to you in recyclable bags instead of the usual plastic, heat-sealed bags. To find out more about this site and about lots of other Internet sources for ordering products online, see Sybex's *Pocket Tour of Shopping on the Internet* by Rosalind Resnick and Heidi Anderson.

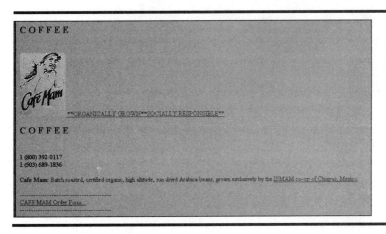

Figure 2.45:
Order organic
coffee beans
grown in
Chiapas,
Mexico, from
Café Mam.

CaPulin Coffee

http://eMall.Com/AshCreek/AshCreek1.html

Another source for coffee beans grown and processed with nonchemical methods is the CaPulin Coffee page (see Figure 2.46). You can order beans that have been grown and dried using traditional methods that don't deprive them of delicate alkaloids crucial to their complex flavor. In addition, a portion of the proceeds from each purchase supports a thriving Mexican cottage industry and protects the rainforests by preventing the clearcutting of them by large commercial coffee-growing enterprises.

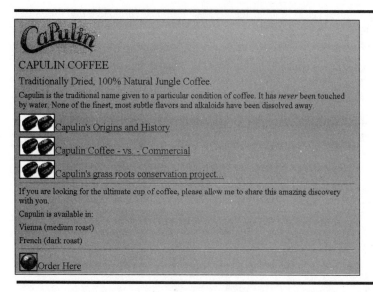

CAPULIN COFFEE
Traditionally Dried, 100% Natural Jungle Coffee.

Capulin is the traditional name given to a particular condition of coffee. It has *never* been touched by water. None of the finest, most subtle flavors and alkaloids have been dissolved away.

Capulin's Origins and History

Capulin Coffee - vs. - Commercial

Capulin's grass roots conservation project...

If you are looking for the ultimate cup of coffee, please allow me to share this amazing discovery with you.

Capulin is available in:

Vienna (medium roast)

French (dark roast)

Order Here

Figure 2.46 : CaPulin Coffee— Mexican cottage industry coffee

Harvard Espresso Company Biotic Diversity Fund

http://www.coffees.com/biotic.html

The objective of the Harvard Espresso Company is to provide a high-quality coffee bean and to use the profits from the business to contribute to the preservation of endangered tropical ecosystems. Figure 2.47 shows the company's home page. This is only one of a number of politically and environmentally conscious services that you can support through the Internet.

TEA

As I sit here with my cup of steaming Celestial Seasonings Morning Thunder tea (a mixture of tea and South American mate, which adds body to the flavor), I am struck by the versatility of this modest beverage. Tea has been with us a good deal longer than coffee and has served many purposes in Asian and European cultures. Drinking tea at a bed-and-breakfast in Devonshire, England, on a rainy morning gave us a sense of walking into a Jane Austen novel.

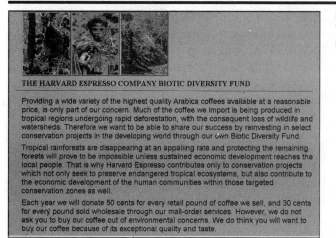

Figure 2.47:
The Harvard Expresso
Company Biodiversity Fund

THE HARVARD ESPRESSO COMPANY BIOTIC DIVERSITY FUND

Providing a wide variety of the highest quality Arabica coffees available at a reasonable price, is only part of our concern. Much of the coffee we import is being produced in tropical regions undergoing rapid deforestation, with the consequent loss of wildlife and watersheds. Therefore we want to be able to share our success by reinvesting in select conservation projects in the developing world through our own Biotic Diversity Fund.

Tropical rainforests are disappearing at an appalling rate and protecting the remaining forests will prove to be impossible unless sustained economic development reaches the local people. That is why Harvard Espresso contributes only to conservation projects which not only seek to preserve endangered tropical ecosystems, but also contribute to the economic development of the human communities within those targeted conservation zones as well.

Each year we will donate 50 cents for every retail pound of coffee we sell, and 30 cents for every pound sold wholesale through our mail-order services. However, we do not ask you to buy our coffee out of environmental concerns. We do think you will want to buy our coffee because of its exceptional quality and taste.

General Tea Information

rec.food.drink.tea

The newsgroup rec.food.drink.tea is in many ways comparable to the general coffee newsgroup, but we must say that the tone here is, well, more refined. The topics of discussion cover which kinds of teas people like the most, how to make the best tea, whether porcelain or metal pots are best, what kind of automatic tea makers are available, and what tea drinkers like to mix in their tea. An informative and comprehensive tea FAQ is referenced by B. Nielsen, who points out that it is a work in progress, located at http://www.daimi.aau.dk/nielsen/tea/teaminifaq.html. In the FAQ are discussions of teabags versus teaballs, starting with cold versus hot water (cold is *definitely* recommended), and a thorough review of a range of teas. Mr. Nielsen has clearly put a lot of effort into this work, and it is worthy of your attention if you are interested in the subject.

The History and Culture of Tea

http://www.daimi.aau.dk/nielsen/tea/teapage.html

In case you haven't given thought to the Boston Tea Party or to the fact that Marcel Proust's madelaine that commences his 2000-page opus *La Recherche du Temps Perdu* is dipped in a cup of tea, you will be reminded

High Tea—Little Known Facts

High tea, known the world over as an English custom, is taken late in the afternoon, as day transposes into evening. Some time for reflection and contemplation is reserved for this beautiful and much neglected portion of the day. Traditional high tea was a hallmark of the working classes in England. They sat at high tables and ate bangers (sausages) while enjoying the company of friends. Tea service on low tables is of the more "civilized" variety—served with tiny crust-trimmed sandwiches (the proverbial cucumber sandwich) to be consumed in two (not one or three) bites. Afternoon tea service is commonly offered at finer hotels in England and can be a way to relax and enjoy the plush surroundings of the upper classes without spending a king's ransom for a room.

of it in the history of tea found in B. Nielsen's Tea page. Even though the Tea page is not graced with a stunning graphical interface or studded with illustrations, the true tea devotee can gain a good deal of information here. A large collection of links to other tea resources is presented, as well as a range of other less closely related subjects. George Orwell shows us some of what a British stiff upper lip is made in his discourse about how tea *should* be made and drunk in George Orwell on tea. You can learn about The history of tea, and there are links to Web pages on Mate (a South American herb that is brewed and drunk like tea) and Water (one of the crucial ingredients in making tea).

A World of Tea

http://www.stashtea.com/~tea

A World of Tea is a site sponsored by the Stash Tea Company (see Figure 2.48), but its history of tea is somewhat more fully realized than that on the Tea page. And the tea-related quotations section is worth browsing if you are partial to English writers.

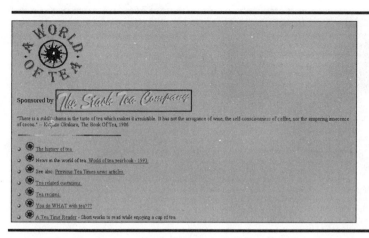

Figure 2.48:
Tea in its many
manifestations—
the Stash Tea
Company's World
of Tea

Celestial Seasonings

http://www.usa.net/celestial/tealist.html

Before we ever had anything other than iced tea, Lipton's tea, or peppermint tea, as bicycle racers we were aware of Celestial Seasonings. The company sponsored the premier American bicycle stage race, the Red Zinger Classic, in the Colorado Rockies. We tried some Red Zinger out of loyalty and didn't know what to think of it. All that has changed, and we regularly enjoy Celestial Seasonings' full range of herbal and caffeinated teas. Morning Thunder provides a great jolt in the morning; a bit of South American mate in it adds some full-bodied flavor. The wide range of zingers—lemon, raspberry, wildberry, and others—are great afternoon drinks that won't keep you awake all night. If you don't have them available locally, you can order them through this Web page (see Figure 2.49).

OTHER BEVERAGES

Perhaps the first thing that leaps to mind when we think of the generic beverage in life is water. In the modern world, a close second has to be Coca-Cola. How many of us can remember going to the barber shop as kids to get a 75-cent haircut, and after we were finished, getting treated to a Coke for a nickel. That's right, folks. It wasn't all that long ago.

Figure 2.49:
Celestial Seasonings tea selection

The Greatest Ambassador for American Culture

alt.food.cocacola

Today, of course, you can't get a Coke for a nickel, but you can get it just about any place in the world. You will find postings in this newsgroup from a number of countries, attesting to the astonishing power of Coca-Cola as a global representative of the U.S. Also, if you are interested in finding out about, or just trading stories about, Coca-Cola memorabilia, you'll want to check out some discussions of this newsgroup. You'll probably be fascinated by a number of other topics of discussion, such as the former cocaine content of Coke and the fact that coca leaves (with the cocaine removed) are still included in the manufacture of Coca-Cola.

Cider Digest Mailing List

cider-request@eklektix.com

Are you a cider enthusiast? If you would like to exchange ideas with others of your kind, send the message SUBSCRIBE to the above address. You will receive a confirmation if your message is successful, and you will begin to get a stream of cider-related messages in your mailbox.

Special Diets

For many reasons, either by choice or by necessity, lots of us undertake to control the food we consume through the discipline of a diet. For some reason, whenever that word is mentioned, the Diet of Worms jumps into my head, and immediately the whole notion of diet is forced into a different arena. Most people didn't have my high school history teacher, though, so they don't carry the same burdens through their lives. The amount of time and money that we spend on diets in the U.S. is staggering, and yet with our increasingly sophisticated methods of determining the effects of what we eat on our lives, it makes more and more sense to educate ourselves about what we eat and control it accordingly. In addition, it is most helpful to be in constant contact with a body of people who are committed to the same dietary practices.

Vegan Action

http://envirolink.org:80/arrs/va/home.html

The self-proclaimed leader of the pack in dietary ideals is the Vegan (pronounced VEE-gun) movement. This is not just a diet, but a lifestyle. The idea here is to live a life in which you consume only vegetable products. Consume here means not only eat, but purchase for use in any way. The Vegan FAQ is an informative document, and you can read it at http://envirolink.org:80/arrs/faqvegan.html. In it you will find out why wearing wool, silk, or leather clothing is a matter of ethical consideration and what you might do to accomplish the vegetarianism of your pet. Vegans are continually scrutinizing every aspect of their lives, and whether or not you feel you want to carry your dietary commitments that far, the facts and observations presented by this critical scrutiny will cause you to pause for thought about our assumptions when we make commonplace decisions about what to wear, what to eat, and what to buy.

On the Vegan Action page (see Figure 2.50), the philosophy is spelled out in detail. Read it to find out what motivates the folks who take this approach to life and how they organize themselves. You can find more about what is behind it all in the FAQ or by subscribing to the Vegan mailing list.

Figure 2.50:
A vegetarian life can bring with it a whole new set of practices and customs.

Vegan Mailing List

listserv@vm.temple.edu

To subscribe to the Vegan mailing list, send an e-mail message to the address above, and in the body of the message, include the following: subscribe vegan-l your name.

After sending this message, you will receive quick confirmation either that you are subscribed to vegan-l (the name of the mailing list) or that a problem occurred with your subscription request because your request had an "UNKNOWN COMMAND," or you may get some other annoying reply. Just take a deep breath and try again, carefully avoiding those UNKNOWN COMMANDS.

When you are successful, you will receive confirmation of your subscription. Shortly after receiving this message, you will begin to receive numerous messages from Vegans all over with information about the contents of products that are acceptable or unacceptable to Vegans and plenty of discussion about the pros and cons of all aspects of the vegetarian life. People frequently request information about how to plan for eating while traveling—either in transit or at their destinations. Folks are also seeking support for continuing with what is sometimes an uphill battle in a culture that seems to assume (in the form of advertising and public information sources) that everyone consumes meat in some form, eggs, and milk.

Whether or not you are vegetarian, you will find the dialogue here spirited and thoughtful. We are not vegetarians, but we find it thought-provoking to take part in this continuing discussion of what we consume and how the food industry affects our lives.

The Error Message

Error messages, as these infamous missives that your computer doesn't know what you're talking about are called, are one of the banes of the computer user's existence. They come in all forms, and most of the time they don't give you much helpful information about how to correct the problem. That's because they are written by software developers or hardware engineers who live in technical worlds that only interface with our world.

When you get an error message, read it and see if it tells you about a problem you understand and can fix. If not, write down the message and acknowledge it (if you are in a Windows program, that means clicking OK). If your system is not restarted, you can go back and try it again. If your system is restarted, you may lose whatever you have been working on since the last time you saved it.

You may get the same error message every time you repeat the event that gave you the first one. That means getting some help from technical support. Many software and hardware compa-

nies keep a tech support staff around (they let them out of their cages to answer the phones during working hours) to help us users with the fixes we get ourselves into, and buried somewhere in your manual (RTFM, remember) may be a phone number, possibly even an 800 number, you can call to talk to a techie. If you get to this point, it is particularly useful to know the exact text of the error message (which you have written down) and to have the other information about your system handy.

Computer companies are finding that the Internet is a useful tool for communicating with users in need of technical support. Rather than waiting on hold for some interminable period of time, you can send a message describing your problem to technical support, who will have time to analyze the problem and research it if necessary before responding to you with a solution. Many companies maintain support forums on the commercial online services (CompuServe, America Online, or Prodigy), and they have pages on the World Wide Web.

Healthy Fast Food for Preschoolers

http://www.umanitoba.ca:80/arrs/VRG/schoolers.html

Is your life graced by the patter of little feet? Do you hear that patter when you are in the kitchen at predictable times of the day, knowing that it means "I'm hungry, and here I come to get something to eat now?" This page (see Figure 2.51), composed by Lisa Rivero, gives a bunch of intelligent suggestions about specific items to offer hungry kids as well as strategies for having them like what you offer them. As we all know, no one has all the answers for every individual, but we like the collection of thoughtful suggestions and methods offered here. These ideas are from a vegetarian perspective, but in our experience with kids, there is much to be said for giving kids food that is easy to digest and mild in flavor. Also, even though we no longer have a preschooler, since ours has evolved into a third-grader, certain dietary habits persist. If we don't give her something to eat by 6:00 PM at the latest, we all pay the price.

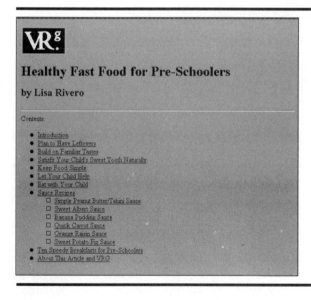

Figure 2.51:
Great ideas for keeping the kids healthy and happy

Food Allergies

http://ificinfo.health.org/fdallmnu.htm

Do you have a food allergy? Do you think you have a food allergy and would like to know what to do about it and how to treat it? The International Food Information Council's Food Allergies page (see Figure 2.52) is a good place to start your research. The process of tracking down the source of an allergy can be dreary and prolonged, and there is a wealth of relevant information about food allergies in general, about which foods are most likely to cause allergies, and about how to treat sensitivities to particular foods.

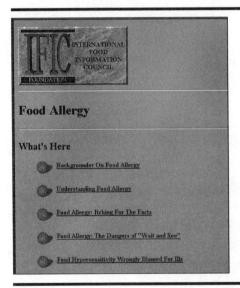

Figure 2.52:
Get some help with food allergies from IFIC's Food Allergy page.

Low-Fat and Fat-Free Foods

alt.food.fat-free

Are you trying to reform your diet or your family's diet so that it is based on low-fat or fat-free foods? If so, you should check out the newsgroup alt.food.fat-free. There is a lively exchange of recipes and products, with lots of standard newsgroup discussion about cooking techniques, diet strategies, and family management suggestions. It was a pleasure to encounter an extended discussion about methods of converting adolescent and preadolescent children to fat-free eating. The discussions about fixing nachos with melted fat-free cheese was so tempting, We can't wait to try it. Other discussions concern how to make your own nonfat yogurt, prepare vinegars flavored with herbs, and microwave potatoes. In general, requests for information are treated with respect and almost always responded to, and there is a lot of encouragement and cheering on of people who are struggling with what can be a difficult change in their lives.

The nature and range of discussion in the closely related alt.food.low-fat is similar. There is an active recipe exchange, as well as information about Web sites that feature information related to dietary control. The Web site http://www.fatfree.com/ is an archive of more than 2000 fat-free recipes that have been collected over time. The archive is organized into sections and is very easy to search.

Fat-Free Mailing List

fatfree-request@hustle.rahul.net

Want to exchange ideas and moral support with others involved with the same efforts you are? To communicate with those kindred spirits, write a message with the text ADD and send it to the address above. Chances are you will be rewarded with a load of responses sooner than you thought possible.

Dining Out

Anyone here who doesn't like to eat out, please raise your hand. OK, don't bother to read this next section. The rest of you—those who spend a significant part of your lives eating at restaurants and loving it—will be delighted to find that a major part of the Internet is dedicated to this passion.

Most newspapers regularly review local restaurants, and bookstores allocate sections to books about restaurants in particular places or of particular types. So why would you want to go to the Internet to find out where to eat when you have so many other resources? If you have ever had any contact with the restaurant business, you know that the rule is volatility, and we're not talking about volatile acids in wine. Most restaurants go out of business in the first year, so clipping a review of a new restaurant and stuffing it in a file for later reference is of limited value. You will want to refer to the Internet to find out what is happening *now*.

Are you about to go on a long-planned, long-anticipated vacation to an exciting location? Are you looking for current information on what and where to eat there? The Net is the place to find it. When we went to Paris in 1984, we were lucky enough to take along Patricia Wells's *Food Lover's Guide to Paris*—a *great* resource. In 1995, when several of our friends were setting off on trips that were to include stays in Paris, we recommended the book. Then we realized that a 1984 edition might not be of much use in 1995. Fortunately, a new edition of *A Food Lover's Guide to Paris* was published in 1993, and so it was still a good reference. But if you want really current information, check out restaurant resources on the Net.

Even if you're traveling to a less exotic location for business or relaxation, you may find yourself in need of restaurant information. The Net has information on restaurants located just about anywhere. Not only can you find recommendations, but you can make recommendations from your own experience for others to use. Chances are that you know about some special places in your city that someone coming from across the world would be most grateful to discover. Many Net sites supply forms for this purpose. You can use them to share your culinary experiences and expertise. After all, who would you be more willing to trust—the jaded palate and sensibility of a paid restaurant critic or the informed opinion of a local resident? (Not that our opinion is biased in any way.) Hearing the opinions and experiences of others in your local restaurants can be particularly entertaining.

Or perhaps you want to take someone to a special place, something out of the norm. Chances are, the Internet can help you.

WIDE-ANGLE RESOURCES

You might want to start by looking at the widest range possible to get a sense of what's out there and how to search for what you want. Some resources start you at the continent level and then let you narrow your search.

The Mother of All Resources

http://www.yahoo.com/Entertainment/Food_and_Eating/Restaurants/Regional_Reviews/

It's never a bad idea to check Yahoo for a topic. You certainly won't come up short here if you are looking for restaurant guides. The range is widely varied at this point, from Milwaukee Dining with it's two links (the Milwaukee Custard List and Unofficial Bars of Milwaukee) to the informative and widely populated Austrian Restaurant Guide.That will most likely change as the number of links here grows over time.

A World Wide Web Dining-Out Menu

http://www.ird.net/diningout.html

Dining Out on the Web is, without a doubt, one of the more impressive resources available on the World Wide Web (see Figure 2.53). It is a true list of lists that is loaded with links to places all over the U.S. and to many other locations throughout the world. The list was originally begun by John Troyer, and the intent is to provide links to guides to restaurants rather than links to reviews or descriptions of individual restaurants. That is not to say that an occasional restaurant review doesn't show up here and there. But you can mainly expect to find a list of sites consisting of many reviews or sometimes just

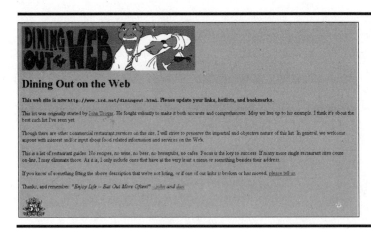

Figure 2.53:
Get ideas about
where to eat on your
next trip from Dining
Out on the Web.

addresses. There is an indication whether the site contains reviews or only listings of restaurants and occasionally a few descriptive words to categorize the site. The sites for major metropolitan areas, for example, Boston, Chicago, New York, San Francisco, New Orleans, and Seattle, have multiple food-oriented listings of various sorts, presumably chosen for usefulness and accuracy. Lots of these sites are fun to look at even if you aren't going there.

All the Restaurants in North America?

http://westweb.com/rest/

The North American Restaurant Guide (see Figure 2.54) should probably be called the U.S. and Canada Restaurant Guide because, for some reason, Mexico is not included. But maybe when the developers came up with a list of more than 300,000 restaurants, they decided to leave Mexico out or do it later.

When you click on the United States Restaurants link, you'll see the map shown in Figure 2.55. Now you click on the state you are interested in, and you get a form that presents you with one box that lists cities and another that lists types of cuisine. Choose one of each and click on SEARCH. When you do that, you will see a menu from which you can choose the state and the type of restaurant. Just for fun, I chose Dallas, Texas, and barbecue and got a list of more than 100 restaurants. There are no reviews here, just addresses.

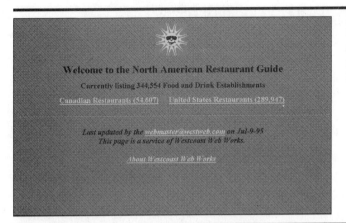

Figure 2.54:
The North American
Restaurant Guide contains
an impressive listing of a
lot of restaurants.

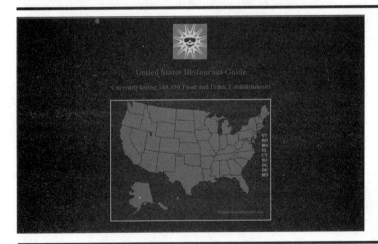

Figure 2.55:
Choose a state by
positioning the
pointer and click-
ing your mouse
button.

A SOMEWHAT NARROWER FOCUS

Once you get a broad view of what is out there on the Net, you will want to refine your focus. Here is a sampling of some lists of restaurants in specific cities.

Lookin' for Bayou Cookin'?

http://tatcom.com/neworl/dining/resttop.html

Having lived a good portion of our young lives in New Orleans, we know that there is a lot more than Cajun and Bayou cooking in the Crescent City. We can remember helping our parents prepare for parties. We pulled the heads off shrimp that our parents cooked up in spicy shrimp boil (Cajun spices) and served to their guests on tables covered with newspapers so that the remaining shells and other debris could be easily contained. Those were the good old days, when Gulf Coast shrimp were available there for 25 cents a pound.

Nonetheless, no one who visits New Orleans comes away untouched by the cuisine. The layers of culture from the Spanish and French periods, as well as the strong Caribbean influence, still can be felt strongly. The New Orleans Virtual Dining Guide (see Figure 2.56) is only one of the links on Dining Out on the Web. At this site you can discover quite a bit about where to go to eat in New Orleans. The multiple sources here are appropriate,

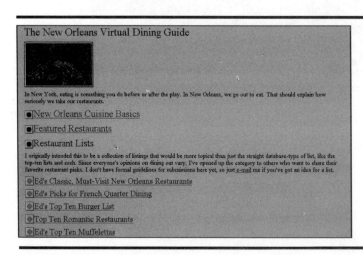

Figure 2.56:
Where to eat in the
Crescent City

because the culinary culture is so rich. You'll want to visit several times, because it takes more than one pass to cover this site.

Boston Serves Up More Than Just Tea

http://genoa.osf.org:8001/boston-food/boston-food.html

You know that a city with as much history as Boston is layered with the many cultures and nationalities that have swept over and through it, each leaving a deposit of its own, like some complex geological process creating a thick layer of sedimentary rock. The Boston Restaurant List will help you sort your way through these layers and decide which to explore. Whether you want the wonders of the North End and its fine Italian restaurants or one of the many famous seafood restaurants found throughout the city, the Boston Restaurant List will be of use.

How Late Will They Deliver?

http://celias.com/celias/index.html

Celia's Chinese Kitchen (see Figure 2.57), one of the first in Boulder, Colorado, to offer online ordering and local delivery, is surely setting a dangerous precedent on the Internet. The extensive menu of more than 200 items is

Figure 2.57: Place your order over the Net.

Celia's Chinese Kitchen

Hours

11:30am-2pm and 5-9pm
Monday thru Saturday
Closed on Sundays

Electronic Chinese Food

Celia's is a new chinese restaurant in east Boulder. They are the first to offer electronic orders on the Web.

Owned and operated by Celia Chen and her family, Celia's Chinese Kitchen provides delicious home style chinese food. The menu includes a wide variety of traditional dishes, Celia's House Specialties, and many vegetarian and low-fat options -- over 210 total selections! The location in the East On Arapahoe shopping center has a lovely dining area and sunny patio for outdoor dining.

Orders may also be placed via email, fax, and phone. Email orders don't need to be in any special format. Just be explicit and provide your phone number. Email orders should be sent to orders@celias.com. An email menu is availble by sending mail to menu@celias.com. Please note that the restaurant staff can **not** respond via email to messages sent to those addresses. You must provide a voice or fax telephone number.

bound to be a temptation to many who would rather have dinner brought to them than to venture out into the cold world of Boulder, Colorado. It has long been a practice for many restaurants to accept orders via the Fax machine. This is the next step. As secure electronic financial transactions become more commonplace, which they no doubt will in the near future, all we'll lack is a virtual delivery service. This is a local service, so if you live much east of Omaha or west of Las Vegas, I wouldn't expect your order to be warm when it arrived.

The Gourmet Ghetto

http://sseos.lbl.gov/Restaurants/Restaurants.html

Not all of Berkeley, California, is known as the Gourmet Ghetto, but a part of it goes by that name. Like much of the San Francisco Bay Area, the interest in restaurants here is intense, and with internationally known establishments such as Chez Panisse and restaurateurs such as Alice Waters, Jeremiah Tower, and Narsai David, the expectation level is high. The Poskanzer family (consisting of Art, Lucille, and their son Harold) has done an impressive job of assembling an inclusive list of the majority of restaurants in Berkeley, with commentary (see Figure 2.58). Browse this list to get a sense of the cultural diversity of which this community is so proud and which is reflected in the range of restaurants here.

Figure 2.58: The wide range of restaurant styles in Berkeley, California

Waiters on Wheels (WOW)

http://sunnyside.com/cgi/get?wow/sf/index

Waiters on Wheels is an online restaurant order and delivery service in San Francisco (see Figure 2.59). At this site, you can choose a meal from the menus of 70 local restaurants, and it will be delivered to your home or office within an hour. The process is simple. Before you place your first order, you supply WOW with some basic information, which is entered into a permanent data bank. Once this is done, all you ever have to do is place your order. Delivery charges are minimal, and for a small additional charge, WOW will stop at your favorite liquor store to pick up a bottle of wine. To make your life even easier, a variety of credit cards are accepted. Corporate accounts are available with bimonthly billing and statements. And now for the good part. Where to eat? The list is extensive, including some of San Francisco's all-time favorites such as Tommaso's, Cadillac Bar, A. Sabella's, Caffe Sport, Gaylord's, and Hunan. Waiters on Wheels is an idea whose time has come, for those of you with everything but time on your hands. Check it out.

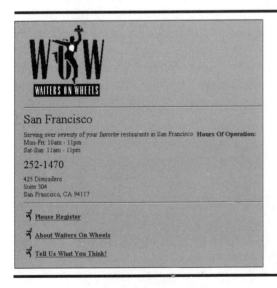

Figure 2.59:
You want it delivered where?

The San Francisco Net

http://www.sf.net/welcome.html

   The San Francisco Net (see Figure 2.60) covers a number of goings on in and around the Bay Area. It takes you from a comprehensive restaurant guide to a listing and review of current cultural events and celebrations. Additionally, the Bay Area's own Anthony Dias Blue brings you in-depth information on wine and spirits, featuring some of his best articles from *Epicure* magazine. Without a doubt, however, the most impressive part of this online tribute to the Bay Area has to be the restaurant reviews. The SF Net undertakes the awesome task of reviewing more than 3200 restaurants in San Francisco and its environs. It does this by accessing the Precision Dining Association, which is an organization of common citizens who scour the area for unique and wonderful places to eat, bringing their cameras, tape recorders, and notebooks to chronicle the high and low points of their meals. Restaurants are rated according to four categories: atmosphere, food quality, service, and overall quality (as many as five stars may be given). The members of the association meet seasonally to consolidate and organize their reviews (read more about it at this Web page). The layout is both easy to follow and attractive. Most are organized by the following four categories: The Best, Alphabetical Order, Type of Cuisine, and What's New. All reviews contain a map of the area, the average cost of a meal, information about reservations, hours, parking, and handicap accessibility. This is no small task. Also at this site you'll find an excellent glossary of food terms, a featured restaurant of

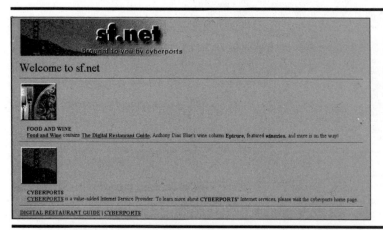

Figure 2.60: An exceptionally complete guide to good eats in the Golden Gate city

Unexpected Costs

You are in charge of organizing a group of 10 people from your office for a lunch at a nice restaurant in honor of a popular co-worker who is leaving. You make the reservation and collect the money in advance. The lunch is a success, and when you get the bill, to your horror, the amount is 15% more than you thought it would be. When making restaurant reservations, it is a good idea to ask if a service charge will be included in the bill. Some restaurants include a 15% charge as a gratuity for the staff, regardless of how many people are in the party. It has been customary for some time at many restaurants to tack on a 15% service charge for parties of six or more, but

don't assume anything—ask when you make the reservation.

Another customary restaurant fee is corkage. If you bring your own bottle of wine to the restaurant, the corkage fee is often about $15.00. Restaurants don't charge this fee because they are mad at you for not buying their wine; it is simply a service charge for supplying the glasses, pouring the wine, ensuring that your glasses are refilled, and washing the glasses when you leave. These are standard operating expenses that the restaurant must cover, and although it may seem as if you are being charged for bringing your own wine, think of yourself as the owner of the restaurant. How would you handle this situation?

the month (including menu and online catering information), and a winery of the month (at the time of this writing, it was the Chalone Group). We have a few recommendations for when you're browsing this site. First, take lots of time to enjoy it. Second, take notes for your next meal out. And third, don't peruse this site on an empty stomach; it could be hazardous to your waistline and to your pocketbook.

Louisville Restaurant Guide

http://www.iglou.com/lou/eats.html

You can satisfy almost any gastronomic craving in Louisville, Kentucky, according to the author of this restaurant guide. The short reviews and thumbnail sketches are provided by Robin Garr—wine and restaurant critic for *The Louisville Times* and *The Courier-Journal* from 1980 to 1990. Mr. Garr's reviews are presented by the Internet Gateway of Louisville (IgLou), and his evaluations are based on a star rating system—four stars being outstanding and no stars being poor. Average pricing of dinner for two and wheelchair accessibility are noted. "New or Noteworthy" restaurant reviews are listed first and change with regularity. Reviews are categorized by type of restaurant, for example, barbecue, Chinese, four star, and so on, and are written in a lively and engaging style. Be sure to follow the link to <u>Robin Garr's Bargain Wine Page</u>. If you want to add a restaurant or a comment about dining in the Louisville area, e-mail Robin Garr on the form provided. As they seem to say in Louisville, Bon appétit, y'all.

Power to the People

http://www.quadralay.com/www/Austin/AustinFood/AustinFood.html

People are passionate about food in Austin, Texas. When it comes to recommendations, commentary, and ordering, they know their baby back ribs from their andouille. Austin Food (see Figure 2.61) is driven by the participants at this site, and they serve up well-thought-out criticism and commentary on the restaurant scene in their fair city. The moderator of this site, Craig Becker, has a witty style and provides a calming voice to the strong opinions of the participants. It's not unusual to find comments at this site

Figure 2.61:
The greater Austin community of restaurant goers is ready to serve you.

such as "I'd rate Cafe Spiazzo a three and a half forker" or "Yech, no! That place is terrible! The food is average at very best, and the atmosphere is incredibly annoying." The bottom line is, if you're looking for a good (or bad) place to eat in Austin, check out Austin Foods.

Tokyo Holiday

http://shrine.cyber.ad.jp:80/~rok/chuo.html

Even if you never go to one of these lovely restaurants, you should read the reviews at this site (see Figure 2.62). These are what restaurant reviews should be. As well as providing the vital statistics such as location, price, credit cards accepted, and hours open, you get true poetry.

Allow us to quote:

"You'll find a meal at Matsunami informal and jolly. Two strides will take you through the tiny garden and into the little entryway of the old wooden house, and two more into the single tatami room where everyone eats. The only furniture in the room is a half dozen tables with grills set into their tops, the bottles of condiments and sauces off the side. One wall is an expanse of windows which rattle in their frames whenever a breeze comes up. The lights are dim, the atmosphere smoky with sesame oil, and everything seems to be quietly crumbling away."

Need we say more? Our thanks to the author, Rick Kennedy.

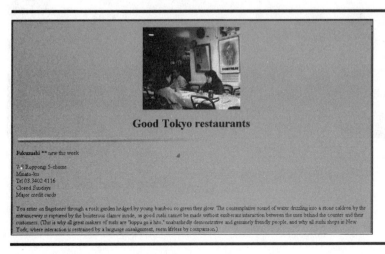

Good Tokyo restaurants

Fukuzushi ** new this week

7-9 Roppongi 5-chome
Minato-ku
Tel 03 3402 4116
Closed Sundays
Major credit cards

You enter on flagstones through a rock garden hedged by young bamboo so green they glow. The contemplative sound of water drizzling into a stone caldron by the entranceway is ruptured by the boisterous clamor inside, as good sushi cannot be made without exuberant interaction between the men behind the counter and their customers. (This is why all great makers of sushi are "kappu ga ii hito," unabashedly demonstrative and genuinely friendly people, and why all sushi shops in New York, where interaction is restrained by a language misalignment, seem lifeless by comparison.)

Figure 2.62:
The guide to good Tokyo restaurants is full of excellent recommendations and even better prose.

Taking Kids Out to Eat, or Are We Having Fun Yet?

Taking kids out to eat can be harrowing. Although the outing is meant to be fun, it often ends with one parent pacing the street outside the restaurant with Haley and the other inside encouraging (are you're teeth clenched yet?) Hannah to hurry up. Fun... Not! Here are a few suggestions for making the experience better.

- Bring something along for the kids to do while waiting for the food to come and while they are waiting for everyone else to finish. (Grown-ups can be so slow.) Try crayons and paper, cards, tape, and scissors. Keep them in a small ziplock bag ready to go for such occasions.

- Order bread right away—don't be too uptight if they fill up on it. You're supposed to be having fun, right?

- Be sure the restaurant you choose is kid friendly, that is, that it serves the basics—buttered noodles, grilled cheese, or something equally as beige and bland.

- Plan on eating and running. Kids don't enjoy lingering over a cup of coffee, so don't expect them to. They may, however, enjoy lingering over a hot fudge sundae. A dinner of bread, ice cream, and hot fudge—the three basic food groups, right? Are they having fun?

- Most kids make a mess. That's why you take them to the restaurant—you don't have to clean up. Well, the waitress or waiter does, so appreciate that by tipping well. He or she deserves it.

If these suggestions don't work (although we think they will), you have three choices: (1) Lower your expectations; (2) hire a baby-sitter; or (3) take Dave Barry's suggestion, "Wait until the kids finish medical school." (By that time, however, you won't be able to afford to go out to eat.) Good luck, and you have our sympathy.

Mostly in Manhattan

http://www.mediabridge.com:80/nyc/dining/

The Food and Dining section of the paperless guide to New York City (see Figure 2.63) gives you the sound bite version of the restaurant review. We'd like to think that's because there are so many restaurants in New York City that you'd only have enough room for brevity; however, we were surprised at how few restaurants are actually listed here. A typical review might read "Uncle Giuseppes Italian Cucina, Superblissimo Italian Fare" or "good food and romantic setting at the former home of Aaron Burr" Is that enough to convince you to go there? Did you always want to know what was for dinner at the former home of Aaron Burr? Not us. This guide would be helpful in general terms, however—for example, if you were on the Lower East Side hankering for a good burrito and didn't know where to go. We're not sure we'd want to invest in some of the higher-priced restaurants, however, without a more complete description. We do think you'll find the City Dining Tips helpful. They give advice on tipping customs, describe the kind of cuisine New York specializes in, and tell you when to avoid a restaurant (there must be a reason it's empty). In short, we would not rely solely on this restaurant guide to such a great and glorious culinary melting pot. Consider it a backup.

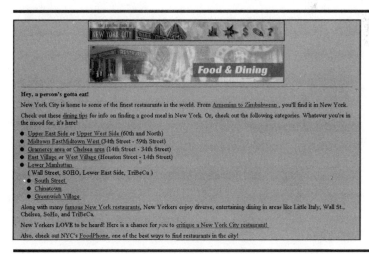

Figure 2.63: The paperless guide to restaurants in New York City focuses mostly on Manhattan.

Kosher Restaurants

http://shamash.nysernet.org/kosher/krestquery.html

Are you going on a trip outside New York and wondering if your destination has even heard of bagels, never mind kosher? Here is a database (see Figure 2.64) that will help you find out about kosher restaurants there. The commentary is not extensive, but there is some discussion beyond location and price in the Kosher Restaurant Database. We're not talking fancy graphics and thousands of links here, but if it's information about kosher restaurants you want, you will find it here.

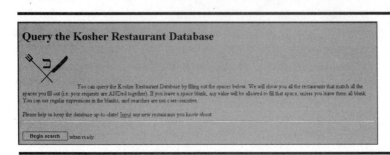

Query the Kosher Restaurant Database

You can query the Kosher Restaurant Database by filling out the spaces below. We will show you all the restaurants that match all the spaces you fill out (i.e. your requests are ANDed together). If you leave a space blank, any value will be allowed to fill that space, unless you leave them all blank. You can use regular expressions in the blanks, and searches are not case-sensitive.

Please help us keep the database up-to-date! Input any new restaurants you know about.

Begin search   when ready.

Figure 2.64:
Well, is it
kosher
already?

A Vegetarian European Holiday

http:// catless.ncl.ac.uk/Vegetarian/

If you are setting off on a trip through Europe, and you are committed to maintaining your vegetarian diet, what would your level of confidence be? With the World Guide to Vegetarian Pages (see Figure 2.65), coordinated by Mr. Geraint Edwards—whose e-mail address is gedge@inner.demon.co.uk—you will stand a much higher chance of maintaining your diet, and doing so in fine culinary fashion. You can find a list of restaurants along with some brief discussion of what you can expect in terms of menu and price. No doubt we can expect the listings to grow as more and more contributors add their commentaries. Europe1 covers Austria, Finland, Italy, Spain, Belgium, France, the Netherlands, Sweden, Cyprus, Germany, Norway, Switzerland, Czechoslovakia, Greece, Poland, Denmark, Hungary, and Portugal. Europe2 covers England, Ireland, Scotland, and Wales.

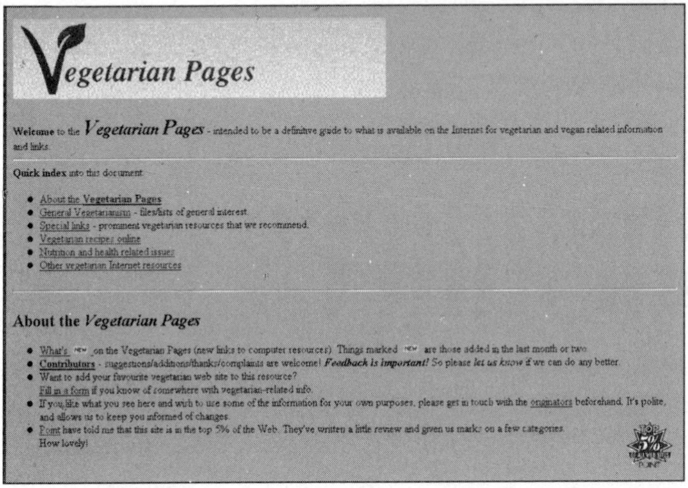

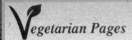

Vegetarian Pages

Welcome to the *Vegetarian Pages* - intended to be a definitive guide to what is available on the Internet for vegetarian and vegan related information and links.

Quick index into this document:

- About the **Vegetarian Pages**
- General Vegetarianism - files/lists of general interest.
- Special links - prominent vegetarian resources that we recommend.
- Vegetarian recipes online
- Nutrition and health related issues
- Other vegetarian Internet resources

About the *Vegetarian Pages*

- What's new on the Vegetarian Pages (new links to computer resources). Things marked new are those added in the last month or two.
- **Contributors** - suggestions/additions/thanks/complaints are welcome! *Feedback is important!* So please let us know if we can do any better.
- Want to add your favourite vegetarian web site to this resource?
  Fill in a form if you know of somewhere with vegetarian-related info.
- If you like what you see here and wish to use some of the information for your own purposes, please get in touch with the originators beforehand. It's polite, and allows us to keep you informed of changes.
- Point have told me that this site is in the top 5% of the Web. They've written a little review and given us marks on a few categories. How lovely!

Figure 2.65:
Enjoy Europe
meat-free.

Appendices

A: Where Do I Go from Here?

B: Internet Service Providers

Where Do I Go from Here?

Now that you know the basics and what's out there on the Internet, you may want to find out more about using the Internet. For example, you may want to learn in more detail about the World Wide Web, Usenet, Gopher, and FTP *and* the software and tools you can use to make the most of your Internet travels. You may be starting your first efforts at home brewing and want to get some pointers from some of the numerous Web pages oriented toward home brewing. Or you may want to compare notes with the bakers that frequent the sourdough newsgroups. Maybe you're ready to take off on a long-awaited vacation and want to get some ideas about what the restaurants will be like when you get there—in that case, almost unlimited resources are at your disposal through the Internet. As soon as you start to look around at the various Net sites, you'll be amazed at what's available.

If you'd like a basic, plain English tour of the Internet and its uses, *Easy Guide to the Internet* by Christian Crumlish is for you. It's like having an Internet guru at your side, explaining everything as you go along. Another great book for newbies is *Access the Internet* by David Peal. This book even includes NetCruiser software, which will get you connected via an easy point-and-click interface in no time.

For an introduction to the World Wide Web, turn to *Surfing the Internet with Netscape* or *Mosaic Access to the Internet*, both by Daniel A. Tauber and Brenda Kienan. Each of these books walks you through getting connected, and they both include the software you need to get started on the Web in a jiffy.

For quick and easy Internet reference, turn to the *Internet Instant Reference* by Paul Hoffman, and for an in-depth overview, try the best-selling *Internet Roadmap* by Bennett Falk. To get familiar with the lingo, you can turn to the compact and concise *Internet Dictionary* by Christian Crumlish.

If you've just got to learn all there is to know about the Internet, the comprehensive *Mastering the Internet* by Glee Harrah Cady and Pat

McGregor is for you. And if you want to find out which tools and utilities are available (often on the Internet itself) to maximize the power of your Internet experience, you'll want to check out *The Internet Tool Kit* by Nancy Cedeno.

All these books have been published by Sybex.

Internet Service Providers

If you need to set up an account with an Internet service provider, this is the place for you. This appendix lists providers in the United States, Canada, Great Britain, Ireland, Australia, and New Zealand.

 The service providers listed here offer full Internet service, including SLIP/PPP accounts, which allow you to use Web browsers such as Mosaic and Netscape.

What's Out There

Three very good sources of information about Internet service providers are available on the Internet itself. Peter Kaminski's Public Dialup Internet Access list (PDIAL) is at ftp://ftp.netcom.com/pub/in/info-deli/public-access/pdial. Yahoo's Internet Access Providers list is at http://www.yahoo.com/Business/COrporations/Internet_Access_providers/. CyberSpace Today's list is at http://www.cybertoday.com/.

This list is by no means comprehensive. It concentrates on service providers that offer national or nearly national Internet service in English-speaking countries. You may prefer to go with a service provider that's local to your area—to minimize your phone bill, it is important to find a service provider that you can access via a local or toll-free phone number.

When you inquire into establishing an account with any of the providers listed in this appendix, tell them the type of account you want—you may want a shell account, if you know and plan to use Unix commands to get around, or you may want the type of point-and-click access that's offered through Netcom's NetCruiser. If you want to run a Web browser such as Mosaic or Netscape, you must have a SLIP or PPP account. Selecting an Internet service provider is a matter of personal preference and local access. Shop around, and if you aren't satisfied at any point, change providers.

IN THE UNITED STATES

In this section we list Internet service providers that provide local access phone numbers in most major American cities. These are the big, national companies. Many areas also have smaller regional Internet providers, which may offer better local access if you're not in a big city. You can find out about these smaller companies by looking in local computer papers such as *MicroTimes* or *Computer Currents* or by getting on the Internet via one of these big companies and checking out the Peter Kaminski, Yahoo, and CyberSpace Today service provider listings.

Netcom Netcom Online Communications Services is a national Internet service provider with local access numbers in most major cities. As of this writing, it has more than 100 local access numbers in the United States and an 800 access number for those who don't live near the local access numbers. Using the 800 number invloves an additional fee. Netcom's NetCruiser software gives you point-and-click access to the Internet. (Netcom also provides a shell account, but stay away from it if you want to run Netscape.) Starting with NetCruiser version 1.6, it is possible to run Netscape on top of NetCruiser. Especially for beginning users who want a point-and-click interface and easy setup of Netscape, this may be a good choice

NetCruiser software is available on disk for free but without documentation at many trade shows and bookstores. It is also available with a very good book, *Access the Internet, Second Edition* (David Peal, Sybex, 1996), that shows you how to use the software. To contact Netcom directly, phone (800) 353-6600 or fax (408) 241-9145.

Performance Systems International (PSINet) Performance Systems International is a national Internet Service Provider with local access numbers in many American cities and in Japan. These folks are currently upgrading their modems to 28.8Kbps, which will give you faster access to the Internet.

To contact PSI directly, phone (800) 82P-SI82 or fax (800) FAXPSI-1.

UUNet/AlterNet UUNet Technologies and AlterNet offer Internet service throughout the United States. They run their own national network.

You can contact UUnet and AlterNet by phone at (800) 488-6383 or by fax at (703) 206-5601.

Portal Portal Communications, Inc., an Internet Service Provider in the San Francisco Bay Area, lets you get connected either by dialing one of its San Francisco Bay Area phone numbers or via the CompuServe network. (This is not CompuServe Information Services, but rather the network on which CompuServe runs.) The CompuServe network, with more than 400 access phone numbers, is a local call from most of the United States.

You can contact Portal by phone at (408) 973-9111 or by fax at (408) 752-1580.

IN CANADA

Listed here are providers that offer access to Internet service in the areas around large Canadian cities. For information about local access in less-populated regions, get connected and check out the Peter Kaminski, Yahoo, and CyberSpace Today lists described earlier in this appendix.

 Many Internet service providers in the U.S. also offer service in Canada and in border towns near Canada. If you're interested and you're in Canada, you can ask some of the big U.S. service providers whether they have a local number near you.

UUNet Canada UUNet Canada is the Canadian division of the United States service provider UUNet/AlterNet, which we described earlier in this appendix. UUNet Canada offers Internet service to large portions of Canada.

You can contact UUNet Canada directly by phone at (416) 368-6621 or by fax at (416) 368-1350.

Internet Direct Internet Direct offers access to folks in the Toronto and Vancouver areas.

You can contact Internet Direct by phone at (604) 691-1600 or by fax at (604) 691-1605.

IN GREAT BRITAIN AND IRELAND

The Internet is, after all, international. Here are some service providers located and offering service in Great Britain and Ireland.

UNet Located in the northwest part of England, with more locations promised, UNet offers access at speeds up to 28.8K, along with various Internet tools for your use.

UNet can be reached by phone at 0925 633 144.

Easynet London-based Easynet provides Internet service throughout England via Pipex, along with a host of Internet tools.

You can reach Easynet by phone at 0171 209 0990.

Ireland On-Line Serving most (if not all) of Ireland, including Belfast, Ireland On-Line offers complete Internet service, including ISDN and leased-line connections.

Contact Ireland On-Line by phone at 00 353 (0)1 8551740.

IN AUSTRALIA AND NEW ZEALAND

Down under in Australia and New Zealand, the Internet is as happening as it is in the northern hemisphere; many terrific sites are located in Australia especially. Here are a couple of service providers for that part of the world.

Connect.com.au In wild and woolly Australia, Internet service (SLIP/PPP) is available from Connect.com.au Pty Ltd.

You can contact the people at Connect.com.au by phone at 61 3 528 2239.

Actrix Actrix Information Exchange offers Internet service (PPP accounts) in the Wellington, New Zealand area.

You can reach these folks by phone at 64 4 389 6316.

Index

Note to the Reader: Throughout this index **boldface** page numbers indicate primary discussions of a topic. Italicized page numbers indicate illustrations.

U

UC Davis page, 102
uk country code, 11
UNet service provider, 152
Uniform Resource Locators (URLs), 19, 25
used computer equipment, 27
Usenet newsgroups, 13–15, *14–15*
UUNet Canada service provider, 151
UUNet service provider, 152

V

Vegan Action, 124–125, *125*
vegan-l list, 125–126
vegetables
    canning, 56
    organic, 46–47
    storing, 47
vegetarian restaurants in Europe, 144, *145*
Virtual Kitchen, 72–73, *73*
Virtual Tasting Group, 97, *97*
Virtually New Orleans, 86
VNR-CUL list, 58

W

WAIS (Wide Area Information Service), 19
Waiters on Wheels (WOW), 137, *137*
WANs (Wide Area Networks), 2
Web Crawler resource, 21

Wells, Patricia, 130
white chocolate, 69
Wide Area Information Service (WAIS), 19
Wide Area Networks (WANs), 2
Wine Page, 97, *97*
wines, **95–102**
    names for, **101**
    pairing with food, **48–49**
    sediment in, **94–95**
World Guide to Vegetarian Pages, 144, *145*
World Wide Web (WWW), 8, *9*, 19–20, *20–22*, *22*–**25**, *24*, 32
World Wide Web Virtual Library, 110
World Wide Web Worm resource, 21

Y

Yahoo tool, **19–20**, *20–21*
    for beer, 104
    for coffee, 113
    for restaurants, 131
Yahoo's Internet Access Providers list, 149
YellowPages resource, 21

Z

ZIP format, 18

The Complete Pocket Tour Series from Sybex

A Pocket Tour of:

Food & Drink on the Internet

Games on the Internet

Health & Fitness on the Internet

Kidstuff on the Internet

Law on the Internet

Money on the Internet

Music on the Internet

Shopping on the Internet

Sports on the Internet

Travel on the Internet

with more coming soon to a store near you.